Women's Education

MAGGIE COATS

The Society for Research into Higher Education
& Open University Press

Published by SRHE and
Open University Press
Celtic Court
22 Ballmoor
Buckingham
MK18 1XW

and
1900 Frost Road, Suite 101
Bristol, PA 19007, USA

First Published 1994

A catalogue record of this book is available from the British Library.

ISBN 0 335 15734 3 (pb)   0 335 15735 1 (hb)

Library of Congress Cataloging-in-Publication Data
Coats, Maggie, 1940–
    Women's education / Maggie Coats.
        p.   cm. — (The Cutting edge)
    Includes bibliographical references (p.) and index.
    ISBN 0–335–15735–1 ISBN 0–335–15734–3 (pbk.)
        1. Women—Education—Great Britain.   2. Women—Education—Great Britain—
Curricula.   3. Feminism and education—Great Britain.   I. Title.   II. Series:
Cutting edge (Buckingham, England)
LC2042.C63   1993
376'.941—dc20
                                                                      93-11334
                                                                         CIP

Typeset by Graphicraft Typesetters Ltd, Hong Kong
Printed in Great Britain by St Edmundsbury Press Ltd,
Bury St Edmunds, Suffolk

Contents

Series Editor's Introduction

The Cutting Edge series was established to examine how developments related to access and continuing education, in their broadest sense, can throw into sharp relief questions that become fundamental to a changing higher education system.

This book celebrates the achievements of women's education: that is, education designed and provided by women for women, and focused on the needs and experience of women. The author fills a number of gaps in the literature. Her analysis of the development and characteristics of women's education breaks new ground. The case studies of such provision – which form the backbone of the book – give a deeper meaning and substance to notions of access and student centred education than is often the case. They also illustrate the spurious nature of 'content versus process' arguments in such educational debates. Just as the left or right hemispheres of our brains operate in concert to shape our experience of the world, content and process dimensions of education are fused when women's needs and experiences are placed at the centre of inquiry. Equally, the possibilities of less rigid understandings of divisions between education and training, between further and higher education are captured here.

Of particular value is the author's straightforward approach to issues of assessment and progression. She demonstrates how these need not detract from education that places emphasis and value on personal experience and collaborative learning. What is critical is the nature of the relationships and guidance provided.

The author locates her work in the context of feminist ideologies. It would be unfortunate if this were to lead to a dismissal of the rich offerings provided here as somehow peripheral to mainstream concerns. This book is not only relevant but timely. It is being published during a period of unprecedented change in UK higher education. The extension of educational opportunity to groups who have traditionally been under-represented in HE is on the national agenda. Access has become the 'mission cornerstone' for many of the newer universities. Government rhetoric places considerable emphasis on opportunities for women – in education, at work. Many policies, however, work against such aims. Access by women to education, as well as to women's education, is still riddled with obstacles, which are analysed here in some detail. This will continue to be the case as long as concerns with price take precedence over concerns about long-term social costs.

Pressures are mounting against speaking of the need for women's education, much less arguing for its distinctive value. This book provides access to a deeper understanding of the challenges and constraints posed to those who provide opportunities for women and yet, are kept at the margins. The questions it raises are, however, fundamental to current mainstream debate.

Susan Weil

Acknowledgements

When I had finished writing this book I sat down to make a list of all the people who had contributed to it in any way. I wanted to thank all the students, tutors, providers of women's education, members of groups and networks with whom I had worked over the past twenty years. I wanted to acknowledge the help and encouragement given to me by colleagues and friends. There were, however, two problems. First, the list became far longer than the space available and second, as it grew, I became anxious lest I left out anyone. So I have no option but to publicly record my gratitude and affection for all those involved in women's education with whom I have worked and who have contributed to this book.

Three groups of people deserve to be named. From the pages of the book and the entries in the bibliography it will become evident that the NIACE Replan programme had a major impact on women's education. I want to acknowledge the contribution of all those who were involved at that time in working to expand and improve educational opportunities for unwaged women and to thank particularly those members of the Replan National Women's Planning Group for their sisterhood and support.

Growing from that group but separate to it, was another initiative which had a profound influence on me, and that was working with Gill Goodchild and Joyce Deere on the FEU funded research project which examined the curriculum of women-only provision. The central chapters of this book draw directly on the work we did together and I am grateful to them for permission to include it here. I would also like to thank all the students and tutors who took part in that project. They cannot be identified but their contributions are acknowledged.

Finally I want to thank all those close to me who have supported me in many different ways in the production of this book. I thank also Susan Weil, the series editor who encouraged me to write it, and the staff of the Open University Press who have been so patient and helpful throughout.

List of Abbreviations

ALBSU	Adult Literacy and Basic Skills Unit
APL	Accreditation of Prior Learning
BTEC	Business and Technical Education Council
C&G	City and Guilds
CNAA	Council for National Academic Awards
CQSW	Certificate of Qualification in Social Work
CSE	Certificate of Secondary Education
DES	Department of Education and Science
EBAE	European Bureau of Adult Education
EC	European Community
EGSA	Educational Guidance Service for Adults
EOC	Equal Opportunities Commission
ESF	European Social Fund
ESL	English as a Second Language
ESOL	English for Speakers of Other Languages
ET	Employment Training
FE	further education
FEFC	Further Education Funding Council
FEU	Further Education Unit
FHE	further and higher education
GCSE	General Certificate of Secondary Education
HE	higher education
ICDE	International Council for Distance Education
JTS	Job Training Scheme
LA	local authority
LEA	local education authority
MSC	Manpower Services Commission
NEBSM	National Examination Board for Supervisory Management
NFER	National Foundation for Educational Research
NIACE	National Institute of Adult Continuing Education
NVQ	National Vocational Qualification
OCF	open college federation
PCAS	Polytechnics Central Admissions System

PPA   Preschool Playgroups Association
RSA   Royal Society for the encouragement of Arts, Manufactures and
         Commerce
RTL   return to learn
SDA   Sex Discrimination Act
TA   Training Agency
TEC   Training and Enterprise Council
TOPS   Training Opportunities Scheme
UCCA   Universities Central Council on Admissions
WAIT   Women's Access to Information Technology
WEA   Workers' Educational Association
WIST   Women into Science and Technology
WLM   Women's Liberation Movement
WNC   Women's National Commission
WOW   Wider Opportunities for Women
WRN   Women Returners' Network
WTC   women's technology centre
WTS   women's training schemes
YTS   Youth Training Scheme

1 | What is Women's Education?

This book is about women's education; it is not about education for women. There is an important difference between the two terms. 'Women's education' is education which is possessed by or owned by women, education which is

- provided by women for women;
- focusing on the needs of women;
- designed for women and about women.

Education for women may encompass all or some of these characteristics but the notion of ownership is not included. 'For women' implies that external providers are in control, deciding what is appropriate for women, recognizing what women have traditionally wanted or appear to have wanted, what women are thought to want and what appeals to women.

Women's education is for women only and designed intentionally for that purpose. Education for women may, by default, be confined to a group of women only but that is not the prime intent. Indeed, all educational provision for adults should include women and recognize the needs of women, but that is not the same as designing provision specifically for women.

The underlying difference between women's education and education for women is not so much in its subject matter or method of delivery, in the type of education provided or the structure of that provision, but in its intent. Women's education starts from a feminist perspective. Although the ideology of the providers may differ in origin, all share a basic recognition of the position of women in society as one of disadvantage and see education as one way of exposing and challenging that disadvantage. Women's education recognizes the experiences of individual women but locates that experience in the wider structure of society. The recognition of *commonality* – that other women in the group have shared or do share the experiences of the individual woman – is another important component of women's education. Women-only groups allow these experiences to be shared and understood.

Choosing to focus this book on women's education as defined above does not imply that other educational opportunities for women at all levels and in all subjects are inappropriate. Women have long been in the majority in many types of education – in adult education, in evening classes, in GCSE and GCE A level courses. To focus on 'women's education' (i.e. women-only education) is not to denigrate or devalue other educational provision in which women participate. Every enrolment event in adult or continuing education shows that there is a demand for those classes which have traditionally appealed to women and in which women predominate. Many enthusiastic and skilled tutors have for years provided a good educational experience for many thousands of women (Nashashibi 1980; Casling 1986), but the focus of education for women is on education; the focus of women's education is on women. Deliberately and consciously, women's education is women-centred.

There is, however, a problem about terminology. The term 'women-only' is problematic for three reasons. First, it implies exclusivity and separatism; any provision which states or implies 'women-only' is effectively saying 'no men'. Some would argue that this is intentional and desirable – a positive claim for women-only space. Others feel that to designate provision as 'for women' is less confrontational than 'women-only'. And, the challenge is often raised, why not courses that are 'men-only'? Why not indeed – the Sex Discrimination Act is so phrased that it allows for provision, on the same terms, for either women or men.

Section 47 of the Sex Discrimination Act (SDA) 1975, which allowed for single sex provision under certain circumstances, was modified by the SDA, 1986. The three conditions under which it was legal to provide single sex training remained the same. Single sex provision can be offered:

(i) if it appears to you that in the preceding 12 months this work has been carried out solely or mainly by members of the opposite sex in Great Britain;

(ii) if it appears to you that in the preceding 12 months particular work has been carried out solely or mainly by one sex in an area within Great Britain;

(iii) to train for employment those who have not been in regular full-time employment for a time because of domestic or family responsibilities.

Training under (iii) could include: courses to develop confidence and basic skills necessary for a return to employment or further training, courses which involve job sampling or work experience, compensatory courses in specific subjects, guidance or counselling for people returning to work.

(EOC 1986)

Even though there are areas of work where men are locally or nationally underrepresented, there have been few courses encouraging them to enter. I have never seen courses called: 'Men into Primary Teaching', 'Men into Nursery Nursing', 'Men into the Caring Professions', or 'Men into Secretarial Jobs'. Men are also entitled to ask for men-only classes when moving from full-time domestic responsibility back into paid employment – courses which are sometimes designated for 'domestic returners'. The number of men in full-time domestic responsibilities is small, however, and this is not the same as provision for men who have been unemployed.

A second objection to designating provision as 'women-only' is that it may alienate some women since they imagine it is run by radical feminists. Indeed, many women students say that the fact that a course is women-only was not a major factor in their choosing it but that, having experienced women-only groups, they are glad that it was all women and now see this situation as preferable. There have been groups which felt uncomfortable with the term 'women' choosing to call themselves, for example, the 'Ladies Education Group' for fear they might be thought too feminist (Coats 1988a). It is strange that no such stigma is attached to the Women's Institutes or Townswomen's Guilds.

The final and much more valid objection to the term 'women-only' or even to designating a course 'for women' is that it suggests that it is appropriate for all women as women, regardless of their particular characteristics or circumstances. Although all women do have certain experiences in common and do face certain disadvantages because they are women, it does not follow that any group of women, as such, will have identical views or needs. Just as the Women's Liberation Movement (WLM) was accused of being dominated by white middle-class women, so women's education has often failed to recognize the specific conditions of black women, working-class women, lesbian women, older women and women with disabilities. As later chapters of this book on the case for, and the characteristics of, women-only provision will argue, this has implications for targeting women, for the practical provision for women and for the curriculum of women's education as a whole.

Alternatives to women-only as a term, such as 'single gender' groups or provision for 'domestic returners', are not acceptable. They tend to obscure the fact that women's education starts from the premise that, in British society, women are disadvantaged in comparison to men and that women's education exists to redress that disadvantage. De-genderizing provision so that it applies equally to women and to men may seem to be in the spirit of equal opportunities but does not recognize the need for positive action or for challenging oppression. The term 'women-only' may not signify that some women are more disadvantaged than others, but it does indicate that women are disadvantaged in comparison to men.

The experiences of women in other kinds of educational provision has been documented elsewhere (Weil 1986; Coats 1988b) and the value of those opportunities well argued. Many women have been successful in higher education, even when the provision was not appropriate to their needs. Other work has examined some specific types of women's education; the bibliography at the end of this book indicates the range of that coverage. However, in this book, I want to take an overview of women's education as defined above, to bring together the various studies that have been produced since the early

1970s. There are several very good reasons for producing a book on women's education at this particular time (that is, the early 1990s), reasons which are well demonstrated in its aims.

The aims of this book

This book sets out to celebrate the achievements of women's education in the past 20 years and to pay tribute to the women who have provided it and participated in it. It recognizes the contributions of policy makers, course providers and part-time tutors in all sectors – voluntary organizations, community and adult education, further and higher education. It attempts to describe and to analyse what is meant by 'women's education' – to examine its development and to identify the distinctive characteristics of it.

This book is written at a time of change, at a point when the need for women's education is being challenged. Women's education is said to be no longer necessary and explained as economically unjustifiable – a luxury we can no longer afford. Its exclusivity is challenged as unfair. Even those who earlier recognized the disadvantaged position of women and supported women-only provision now claim that the arrival of the 'post-feminist' era means that women no longer need positive action or special consideration. These sentiments are based either on ignorance of the actual position of women or a misunderstanding of the real reasons why women-only provision is needed. It may be that the opposition is but an ill-concealed demonstration of the general backlash against women. These are all issues which are explored in this book.

Another reason why the need for women's education is now challenged and why some of the funding for that provision is threatened is that women's education has always recognized and positively encouraged the use of the collective experience of the group. Individual learning has been mediated through group learning and this has implications both for the individual and for the group. In the 1980s and 1990s the dominant ideology of individualism, reflected in changes in both education and training provision, meant that individual needs were prioritized over collective needs – the inevitable consequence of a 'New Right' political ideology and free-market economic principles. Individual competiveness had become desirable; collective and cooperative action was discouraged. Not only was this a reinforcement of traits that had always been considered 'masculine', but it was also a conscious rejection of feminine preferences. Education and training objectives, work ethics, political policies and social arenas all stress the ideology of the individual. As later chapters of this book demonstrate, this emphasis has had serious effects on the legislation, policy and funding of both educational and training provision in the UK – effects which are particularly damaging to women.

Some would argue that the main reason why it is necessary to document and to defend women's education at this time is because of the feared 'backlash' against any progress towards equality or any recognition of the rights of women (Faludi 1992; French 1992; Roberts 1992). Historically, any move towards the emancipation of women has been cyclical – a period of increased awareness and action on behalf of women, followed by a period of antagonism and reaction. While the current argument against positive action is often disguised in explanations of economic demand or directives from those in positions of power, the perceived trend towards equality is seen as a direct threat to men. A backlash is always likely when women are seen to be making a move towards independence. Women's education is no exception, although the antagonism is often concealed or even devious. Changes in legislation and funding mean that provision must be economically viable or cut, but misunderstood notions of equity suggest that some fear the balance may have swung too far in favour of provision for women.

The ideology of the family, always an emotive issue, is raised again. Whether in the context of royal marriages or women returning to work, it is claimed that stability is only possible in a society where women accept their traditional role. Increased sexual abuse and domestic violence are seen not as an indication of women's subordination and oppression but as signs that the structure of society is being weakened by changes in the position of women and their demand for equality.

There is, of course, one anomaly in this depiction. Individualism is based on the premise that all individuals should pursue their own interests and that from this, society as a whole will benefit. But conservatism – still very influential in political thinking and inextricably entwined with liberal ideas – emphasizes the distinctive nature of gender roles, the return to Victorian values, the sanctity of marriage and the importance of the family. As always, the tension affects not only the choices faced by individual women but also the position of women in society as a whole. These tensions also affect the provision of education and training opportunities for women – and most significantly ideas about women's education.

This book is written not only to celebrate the achievements of women's education but also to challenge the current constraints. It argues forcibly for these future developments:

- for an expansion, not contraction, in all provision for women, including women-only education;
- for the moving of women's education in from the margins to the mainstream, recognizing its unique contribution to education;
- for the needs of women to be recognized not as a short-term issue, requiring temporary funding, but as an ongoing response to the particular needs of women requiring secure dedicated funding and permanent provision;
- for the lessons learned from women's education over the past 20 years to be embedded in all education where women participate.

The arguments for women-only provision are based on a recognition of the experiences of women at school and the position of women in society as a whole – which recognizes that women are in a position of disadvantage.

This position shows little sign of changing. Until it does, women's education will play an important compensatory role in preparing individual women to re-enter education, training or employment, in enabling them to move to other areas of work or to reach higher levels of attainment. At the same time it may enable them to discover reasons for their disadvantage and empower them to challenge it.

Women are not a minority – there are more adult women than adult men in the UK today (EOC 1992). There are certainly more women in adult education and in most educational sectors other than higher education. Women are not intellectually inferior to men – many young women perform better at school than young men; more young women stay on at school or enter further education, but fewer women enter higher education or participate in vocational training. Social factors operate against certain groups of women fulfilling their educational potential and being admitted to higher education; working class women, black women and older women are all underrepresented.

This book focuses on the needs of adult women, not of young women or girls, but it is important to remember that all adult women had a gendered educational experience. That experience, maybe some ten to 40 years ago, was possibly more traditional and stereotypical than today. For adult women we have to recognize that there are different needs because of their different expectations and experiences throughout childhood and schooling, their different life cycles and patterns of work, and their different responsibilities in adult life.

It focuses also on the needs of women 'returners' – those women who have been out of paid employment for some years and now wish to return to education, training or paid work. It is for them that women-only provision is most appropriate, although other groups and subjects may benefit from being provided for women-only groups. The term 'returner' suggests a time and process of change, of transition, and this has always been a component of women's education.

The simple pattern of women taking 'time out' from paid work to bear and rear children and then, after several years, returning to employment has been shown to be outdated (Martin and Roberts 1984). Many women still leave paid work at the birth of their first child; some return at the end of maternity leave; others return later. Many women work at least part-time between children, possibly reducing hours or leaving employment for the care of other dependants. Some women move in and out of work as the opportunity arises or because of economic need. Women who leave work entirely usually return to less well paid jobs, often because they are part-time or temporary. All providers of education or training opportunities for women need to recognize this changing pattern of women's life cycles and respond with more flexible patterns than those suggested by a single 'career break'. But whatever their previous education, training or employment experience, many women find that a period of time out of paid work does allow them to reflect on those experiences and to review the future options available to them. It is in assisting this reappraisal and reorientation before or during the re-entry period that women's education has made its most effective contribution.

The format of this book

The gendered pattern of education, training and employment reflected in the statistics in this book has its roots in the past. The structure of the provision of educational opportunities for adults, particularly for women, is based on a historical legacy. To understand women's education today it is necessary to look at its development over time and to trace the strands which can still be identified. Chapter 2 takes this historical perspective.

From an examination of the development of women's education, especially since the early 1970s, it is apparent that the Women's Movement, and associated feminist theories, have made a major impact on present-day provision. Chapter 3 looks at some of the most influential feminist positions, as well as examining other theoretical approaches that have been significant in developing both policy and practice.

Chapter 4 examines the case for women-only provision. Early socialization and gendered school experiences all affect the attainments and aspirations of young women. Society expects certain patterns of behaviour from women and assigns certain tasks to women within marriage, the family and the domestic arena. Many women still conform to these expectations. Women's education seeks to support women yet challenge some of the assumptions underpinning their role. Above all, women-only provision seeks to help women to cope with transition and change. In this chapter the case for women-only education as an option is argued and defended.

In Chapter 5 the whole curriculum of women's education is explored. First the practical considerations are listed, using checklists and guidelines designed by those experienced in its provision. Then the curriculum is analysed in greater detail, using various frameworks to explore the significant characteristics of women's education.

Chapters 6, 7 and 8 look at examples of women's education in practice, drawing on a range of case studies covered in an extensive study of women-only provision (Coats *et al.* 1988). From this study, several major themes emerged and guidelines for good practice were devised.

One area of current concern is discussed in Chapter 9. Although this book is called *Women's Education*, the difference between education and training is not always clear. This chapter looks particularly at women's training since the provision of training opportunities reflects very clearly the way that women are perceived as potential or actual workers. In considering recent and potential changes in women-only training, new patterns are questioned and issues of concern raised.

The final chapter of the book concludes this study of women's education by extending the theme of change. Since much of the funding for women-only training in Britain comes from European sources, a wider view is needed. By looking at the European picture of provision for women, the developments here are set in context. Throughout Europe, changes in policy and practice reflect a changing ideology about women and work, which has a direct impact on women's education.

Change in itself does not have to be resisted, but challenging that change becomes necessary when it threatens to destroy the gains that women have made, the spaces they have created, the provision they have designed. If there is a backlash against women then women-only provision becomes an obvious target. The real motives for change have to be exposed and women's education defended.

2 | The Background to Women's Education Today

The pattern of women's education as it exists in Great Britain today is mainly the result of developments since the early 1970s, but its roots lie further in the past. To understand this development it is necessary to look briefly at the history of adult education as a whole and provision for women in particular. To focus on adult education only, however, would be to miss an important component. Women's education, as a response to the needs of women today, has to recognize the legacy of women's earlier educational experiences, in particular their initial schooling. Their school experiences also reflect ideologies about women which were prevalent at the time. Therefore, this chapter has two distinct but related threads. First it looks at the historical roots of education for women and girls. Second, it looks in more detail at the growth of women's education, as defined in the last chapter, since the early 1970s.

The historical roots of education for women and girls

It is not necessary to recount the history of adult education in detail, but it is important to remember that the education of adults is not new. Like the history of education as a whole, it is rooted in religion, particularly in a concern by various church organizations that people should be able to read the Bible for themselves. Kelly (1970) gives a very useful account of this, particularly of social movements in the nineteenth and early twentieth centuries.

An overview of the history of education for adults shows several class-based strands that are still significant today. For example,

- middle-class liberal provision of education for their own members, especially women denied the conventional openings (e.g. university extramural lectures);
- middle-class provision imposed on the working class, both liberal (e.g. Mechanics Institutes) and compensatory (e.g. Sunday schools for literacy);
- radical provision for the working class, through trade unions and cooperative movements (e.g. the Chartists).

Kelly (1983) summarizes this neatly under five headings:

- education for salvation
- education for vocation
- education for civilization
- education for participation
- education for recreation.

Each of these themes can still be traced in present-day provision for adults, but present-day provision owes much to the recognition that the education of adults is not only necessary but can be instrumental in achieving desired ends.

For women, the earliest educational provision echoed three themes – for reading (the Bible), for their domestic role (Schools for Mothers), and for more radical ends (the Women's Cooperative Guild).

> The first school specifically for adults was a Sunday school for working women established in Nottingham in the year 1798. It ran from 7.00 till 9.00 in the morning and taught Bible reading, writing and arithmetic.
>
> (Kelly 1983)

That same spirit that motivated women to attend school before the duties of the day can still be seen in the lives of many women today, who fit their studies into the early or late hours to avoid clashes with work or family demands.

The fact that women have always had to struggle for education, particularly for adult education, is well documented by Purvis (1980) and others. The pervasive influence of the 'domestic ideology' that encouraged learning only when it was to enhance their role as homemakers can be traced historically and seen reflected in present-day provision. From being allowed to attend Bible reading classes in the Sunday schools, women struggled to be admitted to Mechanics Institutes and the new Working Men's Colleges, to found Working Women's Colleges. When separate provision was made for them, however, often it was in the traditional 'female' skills (Hughes 1991a).

One very clear example of how education for women was provided by others, based on a middle-class perception of what was needed for working-class women, was in the classes provided for mothers during the early years of this century (Davin 1978; Hughes 1991a). When it was discovered that the men recruited to fight in the Boer War were not fit and well nourished, blame was placed, not on their impoverished backgrounds, but on their mothers' ignorance of nutrition and childcare. 'Schools for mothers' became a popular slogan, with better informed middle-class women giving advice and guidance to working-class mothers. The fact that working-class women had to work long hours to provide enough to feed their families and manage on very limited financial resources was not seen as a contributing factor. Educating the mothers was seen as the solution.

Two major movements did provide non-domestic classes that were of direct educational benefit to women. For middle-class women, attending an extramural lecture or class opened up areas of study that sometimes had long-term implications (Brittain 1933). In providing an acceptable alternative to enforced idleness or the practice of accomplishments, these classes allowed women a glimpse of the academic world only available to their brothers. For the working-class woman, the Women's Cooperative Guild could enable her to gain both knowledge and confidence: 'It is impossible to say how much I owe to the Guild. It gave me education and recreation . . . from a shy nervous woman the Guild made me a fighter' (quoted in Davies 1977). This kind of personal change is well documented in contemporary accounts of education provision specifically for women. Again the roots of the past are evident in the provision of the present. So too is the tension between education as liberal or education as improving, between education for conformity or for radical ends.

Just as some provision for adult women emphasized their domestic role, similar ideas influenced the education of working-class girls in school, with an emphasis on housewifery and other domestic subjects so that they would become good maids and mothers. This led to increased provision in child care and what came later to be called domestic 'science'. Middle-class girls, like middle-class mothers, did not need such instruction – their education was in accomplishments rather than necessities, although it may have included the managing of the household and the keeping of accounts.

Throughout the twentieth century, the education of girls has been considered something of a problem – how much? what type? for whom? to what end? On the one hand there was an awareness that girls' attainment differed from that of boys, both in level and in subject. This was recognized as a problem that could and should be solved. How to get more girls to do maths and science was addressed in a 1923 report (Board of Education 1923) and echoed again in a 1975 survey (DES 1975). On the other hand, there was also a reactionary theme that consistently appeared until very recently – how to prepare girls for their main vocation as wives and mothers. To solve this dilemma the other variable was used – that of social class (Delamont and Duffin 1978). Although often disguised as 'ability', most of the 'able' girls in selective schools or streams were from middle-class families. These girls were not expected to be too bothered about domestic skills but were encouraged to prepare for a career. Their task was to achieve academically whilst not losing their femininity; although prepared for a career, the reality was that they would probably spend more years in domestic activities than in employment. Working-class girls in less academic schools and lower streams were not expected to prepare for work – any of the traditional semi-skilled women's jobs would do. These girls were expected to learn skills for their future domestic role, no matter that for them the reality would be a dual role, for all or at least part of their lives.

Education for adult women also reflected class differences. The provision in traditional adult education reflected the interests and concerns of the middle-class housewife – in domestic skills (e.g. cookery, soft furnishing and flower arranging); in the importance of appearance (e.g. dress making, keeping fit);

and in accomplishments (languages, painting etc.). The prospectus for the 1992–3 classes at a local college shows that little has changed. All the classes listed above are on offer and will be attended mainly by women, but there is a difference. Alongside these classes there is provision for educational guidance, return to learn, second chance education and an access programme. A few years ago there was also provision specifically for women – but this has disappeared, although good crèche and playgroup facilities remain. These other facilities are the product of developments in adult education and in women's education over the past 20 years. It is the move from education for women to women's education that is relevant here.

The background to women-only education

As I have shown, the idea that some educational provision should be for women only is not new – indeed, until earlier this century it was inconceivable that any provision for women could be other than in single sex groups. Yet when women in recent years have asked for separate and different educational provision, this has on occasion been treated with suspicion and even hostility.

When provision was seen as suitable in both style and content – provision by women, for women, about issues that affect women – it was acceptable. The same acceptance has always been extended to women-only organizations like the Women's Institute and Townswomen's Guild, which provide both social and educational experiences for many women. It is the growth of feminist women-only educational opportunities since the early 1970s which have been viewed as a threat and received differently.

Looking at the growth of women-only provision in both the United States and Europe, two major influences can be detected. On the one hand there has been a marked, and generally acceptable, extension in the educational opportunities available to all adults, with the growth of continuing education provision generally and the need for more adult training options. However, the demand that some of this provision, both in education and training, should be specifically and exclusively for women has not been so generally welcomed. The effects of the Women's Liberation Movement, the upsurge in feminist thought and action and the equality demands of the 1970s have all had an effect and there has been an increase in women-only opportunities. It is difficult to disentangle the various factors which have contributed to this but demographic, economic, political and educational changes are all significant.

The drop in the birth rate in most western countries has meant that women generally have fewer children and spend fewer years in child bearing and child rearing. Although cultural norms vary in the different countries of Europe, all have seen changes in the pattern of paid employment and unpaid domestic work experienced by most women (EOC 1992). Rises in the rate of separation and divorce, together with remarriage and the numbers of 'lone parents' (most of whom are women) have changed both the attitudes and experiences of women in general. Men's attitudes, experiences and indeed expectations – both for themselves and for women – have not changed to the same extent. Alongside the demographic changes, the economic growth of the post-war years, the demand for labour in the 1960s, and subsequent recession of the 1970s and 1980s, have all affected the amount and type of employment available to women. The influence of feminism and the demand for greater equality of opportunity for women, the legislation from Europe and the creation of the Equal Opportunities Commission all combined to change the educational, training and employment opportunities available for women. Although many would claim that the political and legal changes have been slow and inadequate, the Sex Discrimination Act and the Equal Pay Act of 1975 have provided a framework which affects the entitlement of women.

Against the background of demographic, economic and political change, it can be claimed that some of the most influential evidence has come from research into the experience and expectations of girls at school. Research into the effects of mixed schooling (Byrne 1978; Spender 1982; Arnot 1983; Deem 1984) and into the options and post-school choices of young women (Hunt and Rauta 1975; Bennett and Carter 1983; Licht and Dweck 1983) challenged the assumption of equality of opportunity and exposed discrimination. This made it easier to argue for specific educational provision for women, on the grounds of compensatory need and the full use of individual potential and national resources.

Research and debates within adult education have also used compensatory arguments but one of the major influences on educational and training provision for adults in recent years has been the level of unemployment and, increasingly, the skill shortage. In the late 1980s the initiatives supported by the DES-funded Replan programme explored the needs of the unemployed and unwaged. In particular the needs of unwaged women were addressed through courses and conferences, policy recommendations and publications (NIACE/Replan 1987, 1990, 1991a, b, c). More recently, the projected fall by one third of the 16 to 19 age group has further influenced both planning and provision.

Provision for women in both education and training can be seen to have been influenced by all these factors, but one other major influence has been British membership of the European Community.

The British experience in the context of Europe

Women-only educational provision in Britain drew on work that was already established in the United States and Europe. Hootsmans (1980) provided a useful summary of the developments up to that date, focusing on opportunities available for what she terms 're-entry' women. Surveying provision in Europe she identified the following categories:

- courses stressing social-cultural orientation (such as women's studies);
- courses leading to qualifications or diplomas at the secondary school or university level (to compensate for earlier missed opportunities);
- courses for (re)entry to work or study (reorientation courses such as Retraveiller in France and Wider Opportunities for Women in Britain);
- vocational training, especially in non-traditional fields (such as those funded by the European Social Fund);
- management and leadership training (then little developed in Europe but popular in the United States).

Such programmes were needed, Hootsmanns argued:

> to give women strength, self-confidence and qualifications. Women have spent their lives in learning – but learning in a different way than have men, including their own growth through raising of children. Despite the competencies learned in child rearing and home management, most women return to the labour market or to further study with a sense of fear and trembling. Their former education has been either inadequate or untested or even outdated by technological and economic changes./

The Retraveiller programme in France, initiated in 1973 by Evelyn Sullerot, provided a model for other reorientation and 'return to work' courses. Although more highly structured than similar British provision and serving mostly women with good educational qualifications, it was widely available throughout France and claimed a high 'success' rate. In a publication for the European Community, Sullerot (1987) makes the following points about provision for re-entry women:

- that the initial stage should be for women only;
- that there should be a supported follow-up period after placement in work;
- that women entering non-traditional work has a poor record and many women leave;
- that training should be for entry to work with a future;
- that there is increasing competition between women with similar qualifications for limited jobs;
- that in new technology women are still at the bottom.

With reference to the overall provision for re-entry women in Europe, another study for the European Commission (Challude and Lisien-Norman 1987) provided a comprehensive list of what was available and a series of recommendations to member states. These included:

- Ensure that there is institutional and social recognition of the needs of women returners; where necessary change regulations, classifications and age limits to accommodate them.
- Create a permanent information structure to provide a data bank, lead information campaigns and organize symposia.
- Promote specific research on women returners to provide statistics and studies.

- Develop more and diverse training projects, with training for instructors as necessary.
- Take action at the level of the 'placement authorities', with equality counsellors and training for officers.
- Give 'initiatives' the means (resourcing) to fulfil their role.
- Action needed on the employer's side, such as reintegration projects, removing barriers and retraining as needed.
- Action needed by trade unions by accepting minimum contributions from returning women and taking account of their years before the 'break'.
- Enhance the occupational side of training and increase contacts with work.
- Ensure that an interrupted career does not mean a total break with the working world.

Although these recommendations from the Challude study appear reasonable and achievable, effecting change within member countries is not simply a matter of issuing requirements, many of which still have to be addressed. However, to reinforce the argument that women re-entering the labour market do have particular needs which must be recognized and that women-only provision is necessary, the following statements are taken from a Commission Recommendation on Vocational Training for Women (European Commission 1987):

The Commission of the European Communities recommends as follows

Article 1: It is recommended that the Member States should adopt a policy designed to encourage the participation of young and adult women in training schemes, especially those relevant to occupations of the future, and should develop specific measures, particularly as regards training for occupations where women are under-represented.

Article 2: It is recommended that the Member States should introduce, continue or encourage active measures to [from among the many recommendations on training for women listed]:

2(j) provide specific courses for certain categories of women, particularly underprivileged women and women returning to work after an interruption, particularly in the confidence-building, awareness or pre-training phases;

2(m) introduce support measures such as the provision of flexible childminding arrangements and the establishment of the appropriate social infrastructures so as to enable mothers to take part in training schemes, the introduction of financial incentives or the payment of allowances during training;

2(n) recognize skills acquired in running a household and looking after a family (exemption from certain course elements etc.).

These examples from Europe are important since they expose the gaps between those who realize what should be provided and the lack of that provision. It is widely accepted that equal opportunities legislation in Great Britain was finally agreed in response to pressures from Europe. It is certainly true that much of the women-only provision originated under European initiatives and with funding from the European Social Fund.

The development of women-only provision in Britain

Compensatory education opportunities for adults in general, such as the Fresh Horizons course at the City Lit in London (started in 1966) (Hutchinson 1978), had shown that there was a demand for 'second chance' provision, especially from women. But many women needed more than just an opportunity to return to education as such. Their prior underachievement, unwise choices and, particularly, years out of paid work meant that the main need was to regain confidence and to have access to information, advice and guidance about future possibilities. Confidence building and counselling, in addition to study skills and academic content, were the ingredients of the first specific provision for women in Britain – the New Opportunities for Women course (NOW) at Hatfield Polytechnic in 1971 (Michaels 1973). The NOW model has been copied, adapted, extended and renamed in various institutions through Britain since then. (For various accounts of NOW courses see Aird *et al.* 1980; Sharpe 1981; Kirk 1982; Marshall and Johnson 1983; Dolan *et al.* 1984; Hill 1984.)

In addition to the educational institutions and organizations which had begun to offer women-only provision, there were a number of other initiatives. The Manpower Services Commission (MSC), through its TOPS programme, originally addressed the needs of women by providing training and updating in areas that were traditionally 'women's work', even though they made some effort to recruit women to non-traditional fields also. Their Wider Opportunities scheme experimented in provision specifically for women and 'Wider Opportunities for Women' courses were piloted in Birmingham and Cardiff in 1978 (Fairbairns 1979). These WOW courses became the model for many others which followed, using MSC funding. Unfortunately, the changes implemented in 1988, with the transformation of the MSC to the Training Commission/Agency and the all-embracing 'Employment Training' scheme, left the future of WOW provision in doubt. It seemed ironic that, just as the specific needs of women were recognized and their future importance in the labour market indicated, the one government-funded provision available to them should be withdrawn.

A second type of women-only provision appeared in the following period, in addition to the reorientation courses which provided for 'women returners' such as NOW and WOW. Following the example of other European countries, initiatives started which offered training to women in skills which had traditionally been associated with men, for example, manual trades (building trades like carpentry, plumbing and painting/decorating), as well as motor mechanics, HGV driving and newer skills in electronics and computing. Much of this non-traditional provision was funded by grants from the European Social Fund, although matched funding was required. Thus non-traditional workshops for women were set up, some as independent units and others within colleges of further education. Since local authority funding for this kind of initiative was needed, the provision exists (or existed) mainly in urban areas.

In the 1980s, women-only provision of another kind started, aiming to enable women to progress higher within organizations and careers. In addition to the 'career break' schemes set up by some major employers, positive action courses such as 'Women into Management' have been initiated, both for those in employment and for those wishing to return.

As the effects of the so-called 'career break' become known, the past few years have seen a great expansion in the number of 'updating' courses for women wishing to return to employment. This kind of provision seeks to update the skills that women already have from their previous training or experience. Some are courses in 'professional updating', mainly for graduates or those with qualifications in teaching, accountancy, law etc. Others provide for the updating of skills, such as word processing for typists and former secretaries, or training in new techniques in hairdressing.

While such provision is to be welcomed in that it encourages women to return to employment with greater confidence, it is appropriate only for those women who already have some skills or qualifications and who wish to return to the same kind of work in which they were engaged previously. It also assumes that work is locally available for women with these updated skills.

Thus women-only education and training in Britain covers four major fields:

- reorientation courses for women returning to paid employment after some years of 'domestic responsibility' to compensate for initial underachievement or to allow for a change in direction, updating and preparation for return; these courses may be either 'return to study' or 'return to work' in emphasis, although women are encouraged to look at all the possible options;
- courses in what are usually termed 'non-traditional skills', to allow women to start from a basic level without competition from men, to share with other women doing the same thing and to benefit from women role models;
- provision to enhance women's advancement in various types of work, such as 'women into management' courses etc., to allow women to discover their full potential and to compensate for existing inequality;
- updating courses for women who already have a qualification or skill in a particular occupation but who are out of touch with recent developments or new equipment in their particular field.

In the Hootsmans article discussed above, two other categories of provision were listed. One of these – women's studies courses – are extensively provided in Britain although most of this provision cannot legally be designated as women-only. The other category – providing an opportunity for women to acquire academic qualifications – has long been available in schools, community colleges, evening classes and various institutions of further and higher education. Few of these so far have been designated for women only, although women have usually been in the majority in such classes and many make use of this re-entry route. (For an in-depth study of women returners, see Coats 1988b.) One women-only re-entry route of this kind which has not been mentioned thus far is the single long-term residential college for women only which provides, amongst other things, a very successful route for women who wish to enter higher education (McLaren 1985).

The increase in the number of 'access' courses that provide an accredited route for adult students into higher education has also allowed many women to re-enter education and gain qualifications. Some of these courses, especially those validated by open college networks, do recognize some women-only courses, although most access provision as such would not qualify for single gender classification, unless it is 'access' into an area of work where women are underrepresented (e.g. Women's Access to Engineering). There is evidence from some access courses that there is a need for some women-only groupings since the reorientation needs of women returning to education are not being met (Jarvis 1992). (One well established and very effective women-only access course, as well as a long-term residential college for women, are included in Chapter 6 as case studies.) It can also be argued that while women-only provision may not be appropriate in higher education generally, the lessons learned from women's education need to be recognized by institutions in the provision they make for their adult students, especially women.

From this survey of the development of women-only provision, it has become apparent that it can take a variety of forms for various different purposes. These are explored further in the following chapters.

3 | Feminist Ideologies and Women's Education

In this chapter I want to look at the various theoretical influences on women's education as demonstrated in the different kinds of provision documented in the previous chapter. This will not be a comprehensive examination of feminist theory as such but rather a consideration of the ideologies which have informed the provision of women's education in its various forms since the early 1970s. As often, when considering both theory and practice, the links are complex; different kinds of provision and even different providers demonstrate the influence of different ideologies. Some providers explicitly acknowledge the influence of particular theories on their work; others seem unaware of the ways that theory informs their practice. However, what most women's education has in common is that it reflects in some way the influence of the Women's Liberation Movement (WLM) in Britain. With roots in the Civil Rights movement in the USA during the 1960s, the WLM in Britain in the 1970s combined several theoretical perspectives. The 'Movement' as such did not exist as an organization but was reflected in a range of activities, events and publications.

The WLM in the 1970s was not a coherent ideological whole. Even those women who were active in organizing events or producing publications held various differing positions, some of which merged, others of which opposed, but within this diversity there was some consensus. Underlying the various and sometimes conflicting strands there was one basic feminist premise – that women are disadvantaged and that something must be done to redress this problem. Steps must be taken to expose this disadvantage, to challenge and correct it. It is impossible to find a single definition of feminism which encompasses all the dimensions of feminist thought; a very useful one was given in an earlier book on women's education by Hughes and Kennedy (1985) as:

(i) it [feminism] pertains to women, including the social and psychological aspects of womanhood as distinct from the seemingly fixed biological aspects;

(ii) it is an acute state of awareness about the nature and experiences of being a woman;

(iii) at different times in history and for different groups of women it has become visible in public struggles over equal rights, emancipation, birth control and sexuality, liberation and sisterhood. Activities around these and other issues create the feminist women's movements of the time;

(iv) feminists have different ideas and ways of achieving the freeing of women depending on their class, race, education and political perspectives.

The terminology differs; disadvantage can be described as inequality or discrimination, or as subordination and oppression. What also varied, according to different theoretical perspectives, were the reasons given for this disadvantage and thus the solutions to it.

Within the various strands that made up feminist theory there were two particularly influential and related techniques for challenging this disadvantage – the argument that 'the personal is the political' and the importance placed on the role of 'consciousness raising'. Both of these became important components of women's education. As the influence of the WLM became apparent, it was obvious that education – both the education of girls at school and the education of adult women – had a critical part to play not only in maintaining or endorsing the position of women but also in exposing and challenging it.

Some providers of women's education began their analyses from one of the various different theoretical positions which explained the position of women in society and thus developed their provision accordingly. Other providers recognized only the need of women for education and responded in practical ways.

Three main strands of feminism can be identified as influential during this period and these are usually described as:

(a) liberal feminism
(b) socialist (or Marxist) feminism
(c) radical feminism.

There are two other very influential approaches which draw on and interact with any or all of the above strands; they are the approach which focuses mainly on the personal development of individual women, and that which makes visible the context of her experience. Both approaches may work together or be addressed separately; both will probably be included in any form of women's education but for some the emphasis is on the 'personal', for others on the 'political'. Examining each of the three main theoretical perspectives in turn enables us to see how and why women's education developed in particular forms.

Liberal feminism

Much of the provision for women had its roots in, or was provided initially by, adult education departments at community, college or university level, where traditions of 'liberal' education were already evident. Into a view of education as a 'good' thing in itself and an idea of education as 'compensatory' came the feminist notion of 'equality'. Education was seen as one way of redressing the disadvantage of women by encouraging individuals to fulfil their potential or of redressing the balance between women and men. Provision which would be acceptable from this perspective included:

- provision encouraging women to compensate for earlier academic failure;
- provision for 'women returners' after a career break or encouraging re-entry into the labour force;
- positive action programmes to reduce both the vertical and horizontal segregation of the work force.

For example, in the first category there may be 'return to learn' courses as well as the traditional GCE/GCSE classes and, more recently, various types of 'access to higher education' provision; in the second category, the 'New Opportunities for Women' courses and, more recently, 'Professional Updating for Women'; in the third category some courses such as 'Women into Management' or 'Women into Non-traditional Jobs'. This is not to suggest that all those involved in such provision necessarily hold a liberal ideology – far from it – but it is possible to argue for this kind of provision from that perspective.

Provision influenced by liberal ideas has the advantage of being reinforced legally and endorsed by European recommendations, in some cases receiving funding from the European Community. Although it tends to concentrate on enabling individual women to redress disadvantage, some provision and some providers have been able to challenge discrimination at a structural level.

Socialist (Marxist) feminism

One of the problems with socialist or Marxist feminist theory is the need to explain the relationship between social divisions based on class and social divisions based on gender. Barratt (1980) summarized four theoretical possibilities:

- gender is completely absorbed by class relations;
- gender divisions form a separate system of oppression from class relations;
- the relation between class and gender can be discovered empirically;
- it is possible to achieve a theoretical reconciliation between gender and class.

It is this last approach that has mainly informed women's education, although individual providers may acknowledge the other positions.

Early socialist and Marxist feminist works on gender, class and education started from the position that education for girls and women has been to serve capital's interests and fulfil capital's needs. As Deem (1978) argued, when they leave school, most women are prepared only or mainly for the traditional role of women – in the home and in the family. This is an entirely satisfactory position for capitalism; workers are cared for by women, new workers are reproduced and reared by women, and women are available for a variety of low paid, unskilled, part-time and probably temporary jobs, in response to the needs for labour at any given time.

Deem (1981) later points out that this is too simple a view and the needs of capital are more complex. Substantial theoretical debate and empirical work has subsequently explored the experiences and expectations of girls at school and young women in the post-school sector (in further and higher education). Far less work has been done on the education of adult women. It is much more difficult to attribute the demand by women for education as simply determined by the needs of capital. It is easier to see the provision of education and training opportunities for women as responding to current economic needs. That argument surfaced again during the 1980s as demographic changes and economic recessions made their effects felt.

Many providers of education for women acknowledge that their funding is affected by economic considerations; some justify the reduction in funding in economic terms. On all kinds of courses for women, tutors provide their students with a socialist definition of the political and ideological context and the way that it affects the position of women and the provision of women's education and training opportunities.

Radical feminism

This approach has much in common with those sections of the WLM which endorse radical feminism and see the position of women in society as a consequence of the domination of men. There has been very little analysis of this perspective in relation to adult education, although it has informed both the politics and practice of women-only provision.

The book by Hughes and Kennedy (1985) and their paper which preceded it (1983), both carry a strong argument in support of women's education from a radical feminist perspective. The authors emphasize the importance of women's studies as a challenge to the curriculum content and methods of traditional education. The influence of the WLM, with its valuing of the personal and its focus on perceived, rather than received, knowledge is acknowledged. It challenges the definition of 'women's education' as understood and reinforced by men as encompassing domestic and recreational subjects which suggest that women are interested only in where they live and what they look like.

They argue that the introduction of women's studies as a serious subject for study raised problems for both providers and participants. Drawing as it did on practices within the WLM, allowing all women to speak, respecting and equally valuing their contributions meant that classes could and did, in effect, become 'consciousness raising' groups. On the other hand, there was a move, particularly in higher education, to get women's studies accepted as a new discipline – an academic subject in its own right. But how can the personal experiences of a woman be 'assessed' while respecting her own perception of them?

Quite clearly, to Hughes and Kennedy, women's education is not just to transmit knowledge and ideas but 'also to provide a space for women in which the process of such discovery and learning builds up their confidence and the empowering of themselves' (1985). Here the merging of women's studies and personal change are articulated. Many of the reorientation courses described above, indeed much of what has come to be described as 'women's education', combine objective knowledge about women with subjective change within women.

Women's education for personal development

In many cases, reorientation provision for women currently engaged in wholly domestic responsibilities has taken on a particular character. As indicated above, the needs of such women are not just for educational input but for personal growth and change. Domestic responsibilities, in our society, are awarded no status and no reward. Although child care may rhetorically be described as an important task, in reality many women find their years of child rearing are isolated, unstimulating and lacking in any form of social recognition. Some women become involved in child-centred organizations and activities and there is a lot of evidence to suggest that such organizations as the Preschool Playgroups Association (PPA) provide a stimulating educational experience for the women involved and possibly a route back into education. Other women find satisfaction in voluntary work, another route back into education and employment for some women. Many women, however, have no experiences or involvement outside of the home, other than social interaction with other mothers, to enliven their day. It is for these women, especially those nearing the end of their full-time child care responsibilities, that New Opportunities for Women (NOW) and Wider Opportunities for Women (WOW) provisions developed.

One major provider of women-only education of this type has been the Workers' Educational Association (WEA). The WEA came into the provision of NOW courses soon after the original course at Hatfield (Aird 1980) although the nature and intent of their provision soon changed. The WEA appeared to be an ideal forum for women's education for a number of reasons:

- the organization was not accountable to a college or local authority and would appear more able to initiate change and experiment;
- the WEA has 'radical' roots and would seem appropriate for challenging ideas and providing for equality;
- most tutors are part-time women who themselves have had similar experiences;

- the ethos of the student directed syllabus and the interactive method of presentation would seem most suitable for women-only provision;
- the WEA has the flexibility to provide daytime classes in various locations as required.

Establishing women's education within the WEA, however, appears to have been a long struggle against tradition, prejudice and overt sexism (Crane 1986). Like most organizations, a male hierarchy makes the decisions and controls progress, even when the majority of grass roots participants are female. However, a number of excellent events and publications document the struggle within the WEA for the establishment and recognition of the validity of women's education (see the WEA 'Breaking Our Silence' series; for example, Tallantyre 1985; Crane 1986; Spendiff 1987; Mann 1988).

It is not just the history of women-only provision within the WEA that is of interest, however, but the particular form it has taken. The next section of this chapter examines the theory and practice of provision for women which starts from the personal experience of individual women. I focus on the work of women in the WEA because this organization has been prominent in recording their experiences in providing women-only education, in explaining their theoretical approach, and in exchanging examples of good practice.

Within the provision made by the WEA and the various written accounts of it, several themes emerge. The provision is informed by various strands of feminism – liberal, socialist and radical – but it is the focus on the 'personal' rather than the 'political' which seems to have had the greatest influence, in particular, the influence of 'consciousness raising': 'Radical feminist practice then, has given us the ways to initiate, explore and support change, through the analysis of experience, the fostering of collectivity and the development of new strategies' (Spendiff 1987). This kind of education starts from personal experience. The experiences of women are highly valued; the roles of women are recognized and the skills of women are acknowledged. There is no doubt that the oppression of women is made explicit and individuals are encouraged to understand their own experiences in the context of the position of women in society. The way that women's experiences are devalued is emphasized and it is made clear that the 'fault' lies not in the individual woman but in the society of which she is part.

The role of education as a mechanism for change is recognized: 'Education is about nothing if it is not about change, the opportunity to grow, to develop, to enhance one's understanding and, possibly, one's place in the world' (Crane 1986). Personal growth and personal change are the key features of this approach;

> What is important is that one of the aims of education should be to commence the process of getting to know the self. If the student begins to understand herself, her needs, her fears, her positive and negative aspects, she can then start to contemplate the prospects of making changes that will ultimately improve her life.
>
> (Mann 1988)

The importance of counselling is acknowledged; the inclusion of counselling in the course is named and timetabled. Women are encouraged to reassess their position and to make plans for the future. Each must find and follow her own path – no right route is prescribed. The Rogerian approach of non-directive counselling is accepted and no woman is criticized even when her choice seems reactionary. Counselling should be both individual and within the group, and should include both an 'academic' evaluation of ability and a personal reassessment.

As Tallantyre (1985) suggests, the original emphasis in women's education may have been compensatory but, increasingly, the importance of group dynamics has taken precedence. Aird (1980) describes how 'a deep seated change can take place in quite a short time because of the processes of woman-centred groups'. It is the group which gives support and permission to move forward.

According to Aird, women must 'clarify their sense of being in the world' and yet 'regain contact with our inner worlds'. The dependency needs of women are acknowledged and their need for care and support made explicit. From a negative sense of separation, isolation and depression, women move towards a positive sense of autonomy, freedom, control and choice. Again the role of the tutor – and indeed of the group – is made clear in giving permission and confidence to women to change. Tutors become 'the holders of feelings' (Tallantyre 1985).

Tutors on NOW courses have a difficult and sensitive role to perform. According to Tallantyre (1985) they are not just teachers but 'nurturers of individual development', sharers of women's experiences and role models for the students. Mann's (1988) description of the work of such tutors is almost frightening in its responsibility.

The difficulty in understanding this approach is that the curriculum – its content and methodology – are not made clear. As in all WEA provision, the class itself should decide on the content of the curriculum. As many tutors have discovered, their suggestions – open of course to modification and change – are invariably accepted. Authority cannot be so easily abandoned. Methodology is less problematic and the one message that comes from all the empirical studies is women's relief that the course or class is 'not like school'. Contributions from students are valued and genuine discussion is seen as a learning experience.

Of all those writing about women's education under the name of the WEA, only Barr presents a wider challenge. In the report of a conference held in Durham in 1984, she argues that women's education must be seen as a commitment to social change and to work towards an end to the oppression of women. Not only must women work to maintain the gains they have made but they must move forward to challenge and criticize. She argued that the marginality, the bias against theory and the concentration on similarity rather than difference between women, have inhibited change and must be challenged. In an implicit criticism of some trends in women's education she said: 'Starting from where people are is an excellent starting point but a lousy finishing point. It can often leave them there' (Barr 1984). This is the essence of the criticism of some NOW courses and similar provision. Raising consciousness, increasing confidence, informing women of options for the future is useful only if women have the opportunity, the possibility to move on. To concentrate on personal growth and ignore social constraint is to leave women in danger of an even greater sense of frustration and failure once the course has ended. It can prove a path to a closed and inappropriate dead end (Barr 1984).

Tallantyre (1985) also recognizes the limits of individualism and the need for developing theory: 'We need to develop further theory of our own out of the experience of women to progress significantly beyond individualism'. The gains from the courses which she describes are still more personal than political: a wish to regain and develop a sense of self; to find new perspectives on where women stand and ways of changing it; to find a sense of individual purpose and outlets for creative fulfilment; to acquire confidence and self-esteem to express views; to find ways of relating to and finding support from other women.

Political change, not personal change

Similar criticism is very apparent in the writings of Jane Thompson (1983) and her colleagues at the Women's Education Centre in Southampton (Taking Liberties Collective 1989). For them there are two important spheres of action.

One is to offer women-only, women-centred education which provides women with an education that recognizes and validates their own experiences, especially if they are working-class, black or lesbian women, for example. This education must have an empowering effect, enabling women to make sense of their own lives and giving them a new feminist perspective on the world. Such provision, they argue, should not be seen as giving women a protective environment in which to 'practise' before emerging into the 'real' world of mainstream education; it is a positive educational experience in its own right.

The Taking Liberties Collective argue forcibly that women should not just be prepared for progression to mainstream education but be prepared to challenge it. For radical feminists, all of society, and therefore all of education, is patriarchal – controlled and dominated by white, middle-class, heterosexual men. This is particularly true of higher education, where other groups such as women, the working class, black students and lesbians are seen as 'deviant'. Those from these groups who do manage to cross the barriers of entry must conform to the expected norms, but the answer is to enter and *then* challenge those norms.

Thus women of this perspective are critical of other educational providers who focus on individualism and not collective action. This includes most of adult education, which is male dominated and controlled; most women-only provision, such as the WEA, which they see as operating on a deficiency model of coping or of individual therapy; and non-traditional skills training for women, which leads to dead-end, low paid jobs or no jobs. Such generalized criticism is unfounded but it does serve to remind us of the dangers of individualism and the need to create a collective identity. It echoes the concerns of those involved in radical working-class education (Edwards 1985) who share similar concerns.

Just as the WLM had to move from personal introspection to political action on behalf of women (for example, through rape crisis centres and refuges for victims of domestic violence) so too women's education must address the wider economic, political and social oppression of women if it is really to change the lives of its students. If women-only educational opportunities are to be of real and lasting value for the students concerned, they have to prepare them to move onwards, with confidence, to mainstream provision in education, training or employment. If women-only provision is to have a real impact on education it needs to show just why and how it is successful. This is not to deny that the therapeutic approach which values individual experience is important but, in itself, it is not enough. It does not matter whether tutors place greater emphasis on an analysis which prioritizes the effects of class or of gender, whether they draw on both in an attempt to enable women to make sense of their own individual experiences, or whether they look to informal or formal educational provision to enable women to compensate for earlier failure – and to understand the reasons for that failure.

It seems much more likely that the demand for education by 're-entry women' is a result of various interconnected factors and of considerable struggle on the part of both women providers and women students. Re-entry provision for women, women's studies courses, women's courses in non-traditional areas and women entering higher education as mature students are all sites of struggle, in which liberal feminists, socialist and Marxist feminists and radical feminists have all been engaged. All these theoretical positions can be demonstrated in current women-only provision. To understand the ideology and values which underlie the provision, we need to know something of the range of thinking which informs all the educational opportunities offered to women and to be aware of the debates and the dilemmas involved.

4 | The Case for Women-only Provision

Women's life cycles – a gendered experience

One of the reasons for providing women-only education is that women, as a group, have different expectations and experiences to men. We live in a gendered society, where not only are women's experiences different to those of men but those differences lead to discrimination and disadvantage. This is, of course, a simplistic statement which ignores both the similarities between women and men but also the differences between women themselves. However, the effects of a gendered society are real enough to have significance for education – both the initial education (schooling) of girls and the continuing education of women as (re-entrant) adults.

This chapter looks at the main differences between women and men in terms of two particular spheres – education and employment. I argue that the differences exhibited in these two particular spheres are one reason – one main reason – for providing women-only educational options. I use the word 'options' in this context because not all women will want, need or have access to a women-only alternative. In discussing education and employment patterns I am forced to consider general trends, not individual experiences. The evidence is clear enough, however, to support the argument that many women share similar experiences which may mean that women-only provision is appropriate for them at some stage in their lives.

Gendered socialization begins at birth and is powerfully reinforced during the preschool years. Children starting school at the age of five already have a gendered identity and stereotypical assumptions about the different gendered roles of adults as well as themselves (Chetwynd and Hartnett 1978; Hartnett et al. 1979). Primary school experiences reinforce these assumptions. The organization and staffing of schools, the expectations of attainment and interest, the resources available, the attitudes of teachers and interaction in the classroom all demonstrate that girls receive different 'messages' to boys (French and French 1984).

This continues and is enhanced through secondary schooling, resulting in different achievements and expectations (Delamont 1980; Spender and Sarah 1980; Sutherland 1981; Spender 1982; Whyld 1983). Girls do well at school

– increasingly so; more stay on at school after the minimum leaving age and gain more GCSE and A level passes than boys. Only in the final year do boys appear to overtake the achievements of girls. More boys than girls gain three or more A level passes, which are the crucial requirement for entry to higher education (see Table 4.1). There are marked differences within that achievement, with girls still concentrating on arts, languages and biological sciences and boys concentrating on maths, computing and the physical sciences. There have been some changes over the last few years with more girls taking maths and science subjects at GCSE level although the A level results show a less significant change (see Tables 4.2 and 4.3).

Any discussion of the attainments of girls and boys at school has to take account of the social class of their families. This is not the place for an in-depth analysis of social class and educational achievement, but there is evidence to show that this is still an important determinant of educational success. Proportionally fewer pupils of working-class families stay on at school, continue into further education and into higher education. Working-class girls are far less likely than working-class boys to gain post-school qualifications, either academic or vocational (see Table 4.4).

The choice of subjects for GCSE and A levels along gendered lines is linked to and reflected in choice of career. Although more young women than young men go on into further education, their courses are likely to lead to clerical, catering or caring qualifications. Young women who leave school and enter employment are less likely to have day or block release (see Table 4.5).

Those women who are now re-entering education were educated in a more gendered environment than now; most left school between 10 and 49 years ago. These women are even more likely to have been channelled into stereotypical occupations. In a study of mature women re-entrants to education (Coats 1988b), one main finding was that their education, training and occupations had followed gendered lines. Regardless of the social class of their families of origin, they underachieved. Even when their potential ability had been recognized (for example, by passing the eleven-plus exam and going to grammar school), they tended to be early leavers, either due to family circumstances or disaffection. Very few consciously chose a career. Their one expectation, and particularly the expectation of their family, was that they would work for a while, then marry and have a family – and thus live happily ever after! Unrealistic as it is, this is still the expectation of many young women. Even though the evidence suggests that the 'traditional' family pattern of husband as breadwinner, wife in full-time domestic role with dependent children, now forms a minority of families and that many women will at some time find themselves alone and unsupported, for many young women jobs and careers are not seen as the main priority (see Table 4.6). Given the lack of careers guidance that many women received in the past, especially working-class women, it is not surprising that many saw their years of paid employment between school and child bearing as filling in before their main task began – that of caring for a home and raising a family.

Looking at the wider pattern of the distribution of women and men in the

Table 4.1 GCSE/GCE/CSE qualifications and intended destination of pupils leaving school[1] during 1989–90 in England and Wales (ooos)

| | Intended destination | | | | | | Available for employment[3] | | | All destinations | | |
| | Higher education[2] | | | Further education[2] | | | | | | | | |
	Males	Females	Persons	Males	Females	Persons	Males	Females	Persons	Males	Females	Persons
Qualifications held on leaving school												
Leavers with A level passes												
3 or more	35	32	67	2	2	4	9	9	17	45	43	88
2	8	9	16	1	2	3	7	7	14	16	18	34
1	3	3	6	2	2	4	7	7	13	11	12	23
Total	46	44	90	5	6	11	22	23	45	73	73	146
Leavers with GCSE/O level/CSE alone												
5 or more A–C awards/CSE grade 1	1	1	1	17	27	44	19	21	40	37	49	85
1–4 A–C awards/CSE grade 1	–	1	1	22	32	54	59	53	112	82	85	167
Numbers with 2 or more A level passes	42	41	84	3	4	7	16	16	32	61	62	123
Numbers with at least 5 A–C awards and/or at least 1 A level pass	46	45	91	21	33	55	42	44	85	109	122	231

1 Excluding those leaving from special schools.
2 Previous versions of the table showed groupings for university and further education (including other higher education and teacher training).
3 Including those leaving for temporary employment pending entry to full-time education and with destination not known.
Source: DE (1991)

Table 4.2 Pupils leaving school with GCSE/GCE/O level/SCE grades (A–C) and CSE grade 1 (irrespective of any A levels/H grades obtained) by subject and sex, 1970–90

	England and Wales			Great Britain				1989–90[1]		Number (000s)
	1970–1	1975–6	1980–1	1980–1	1985–6	1988–9	All persons	Males	Females	All persons
	All persons			All persons						
Percentage obtaining GCSE/GCE O level/SCE grades (A–C) and CSE (grade 1) in English	34	36	37	38	41	45	49	42	56	335
History	14	14	15	15	15	16	17	15	18	114
French	15	14	14	15	15	18	20	15	25	136
Music, drama, visual arts	11	13	13	13	14	19	20	15	26	138
Mathematics	23	24	27	29	31	36	37	38	36	251
Physics	10	11	14	14	16	17	17	23	11	116
Chemistry	8	9	12	12	14	16	17	18	15	113
Biology	13	15	16	16	16	17	17	13	21	114
Other science[2]	10	11	11	11	12	16	18	24	12	125
Geography	15	16	16	16	17	18	19	21	18	133
Vocational subjects[3]	7	8	10	11	12	15	16	7	26	110
Any subject	43	50	53	53	55	62	64	60	69	439
English and mathematics	20	20	23	24	27	30	33	32	34	226
English, mathematics and science	16	16	19	19	22	25	28	28	27	191
English, mathematics, science and modern languages	10	10	11	11	12	15	17	15	20	118
ALL LEAVERS (thousands)	613	707	778	865	844	730	682	350	332	682

1 Due to changes in subject classification, direct comparisons of individual subjects are not possible between 1985–6 and 1989–90.
2 Including metal work, woodwork and technical drawing.
3 Including business and domestic subjects.
Source: DE (1991)

Table 4.3 Pupils leaving school with 2 or more GCE A levels/3 or more SCE H grades by subject combinations by subject and sex, 1970–90

	England and Wales			Great Britain						
	1970–1	1975–6	1980–1	1980–1	1985–6	1988–9	1989–90[1]			Numbers (000s)
							All persons	Males	Females	All persons
	All persons			*All persons*						
Percentage obtaining two or more A levels/three or more H grades										
Mathematics/science	23	20	22	20	22	13	11	15	7	15
Mathematics/mixed	8	11	14	21	20	27	26	30	21	36
Total Mathematics	31	31	36	40	42	39	37	45	28	51
English/arts/social studies	33	31	26	25	24	24	25	16	34	35
English/mixed	3	4	5	14	14	13	15	13	17	21
Total English	36	35	31	39	38	36	40	30	51	57
Geography/arts/social studies	14	13	10	10	10	10	10	11	10	15
Geography/mixed	7	9	8	10	11	11	11	13	9	15
Total Geography	21	23	18	20	21	22	21	24	18	30
Science	33	31	32	28	29	16	14	19	9	20
Arts/social studies	51	48	44	40	39	41	42	33	51	59
Mixed[2]	15	21	24	31	32	43	44	48	39	61
All leavers with two or more A levels/three or more H grades (thousands)										
ENGLAND	86	85	99	99	98	107	} 123	} 61	} 62	} 123
WALES	8	5	6	6	6	6				
SCOTLAND	–	–	–	17	17	18	17	8	9	17
GREAT BRITAIN	–	–	–	122	121	131	140	69	71	140

1 Due to changes in subject classification, direct comparisons of individual subjects are not possible between 1985–6 and 1989–90.
2 Science and arts or social studies.
Source: DE (1991)

Table 4.4 Highest qualification level attained[1]: By socio-economic group of father, 1989 in Great Britain (percentages and numbers)

	Professional	Employers and managers	Intermediate and junior non-manual	Skilled manual and own account non-professional	Semi-skilled manual and personal service	Unskilled manual	All persons
Highest qualification level attained							
Degree	38	17	18	5	4	3	11
Higher education	18	16	16	12	7	6	13
A level	10	14	13	9	8	6	10
O level	20	24	27	22	20	14	22
CSE	4	8	9	13	13	13	11
Foreign	5	5	3	3	2	3	3
No qualifications	6	17	14	37	47	54	31
Sample size (= 100%) (numbers)	440	1656	835	3383	1059	438	7811

1 Persons aged 25–49 not in full time education.
Source: CSO (1992)

Table 4.5 Students[1] from home and abroad enrolled in education by type of course, mode of study[2], sex and subject group[3], 1989–90 (000s)

Subject group	Postgraduate level Full-time	Postgraduate level Part-time	First degree Full-time	First degree Part-time	Other higher education[4] Full-time	Other higher education[4] Part-time	Total higher education	Further education[5] Full-time	Further education[5] Part-time	All students Full-time Home	All students Full-time Home and abroad	All students Part-time Home and abroad[6]
Males												
1 Medicine & dentistry	1.6	1.8	12.8	0.1	0.1	0.1	16.5	0.2	0.5	12.8	14.7	2.5
2 Allied medicine	1.0	0.9	3.8	0.5	1.0	1.9	9.1	1.0	4.2	6.0	6.8	7.5
3 Biological sciences	2.8	1.4	10.4	0.5	0.7	0.5	16.4	–	0.3	12.6	13.9	2.8
4 Agriculture	1.1	0.3	3.1	–	1.4	0.2	6.1	4.5	18.7	8.9	10.0	19.2
5 Physical sciences	6.0	1.7	20.4	1.1	1.3	2.5	32.9	0.2	1.7	25.4	27.8	7.0
6 Mathematical sciences	4.1	1.9	23.0	1.4	7.2	6.0	43.4	8.1	22.5	39.2	42.2	31.7
7 Engineering & technology	8.1	4.7	51.3	4.0	12.4	40.2	120.7	30.7	192.0	88.2	102.4	241.0
8 Architecture	1.6	1.7	11.7	2.7	3.6	17.2	38.5	20.0	115.4	34.9	36.8	137.1
9 Social sciences	5.5	3.7	32.7	2.8	2.9	2.8	50.5	1.9	12.3	36.7	43.1	21.6
10 Business & financial studies	4.6	12.7	24.2	3.3	15.1	48.2	108.2	36.1	84.8	73.5	80.0	149.0
11 Library & info. science	0.6	0.3	1.2	–	0.4	0.3	2.8	0.5	1.8	2.4	2.6	2.4
12 Languages	1.5	1.1	11.1	0.3	0.4	1.1	15.5	1.4	40.7	12.3	14.4	43.2
13 Humanities	1.8	2.0	10.0	0.4	0.2	0.3	14.7	–	1.1	10.9	12.0	3.9
14 Creative arts	1.2	0.6	12.4	0.3	5.8	0.6	20.9	18.2	28.2	36.6	37.7	29.6
15 Education[7]	4.6	5.5	4.9	1.1	0.8	3.9	20.8	2.1	19.2	10.5	12.4	29.7
16 Multi-disciplinary studies	0.8	1.0	33.7	2.3	2.6	1.1	41.5	19.7	119.2	52.7	56.8	123.6
17 GCSE, SCE and CSE	–	–	–	–	–	–	–	50.8	100.1	50.0	50.8	100.1
All subjects[8]	46.9	41.5	266.4	20.8	56.1	126.9	558.5	208.4	800.1	526.7	577.7	989.3

Females

Subject group											
1 Medicine & dentistry	1.1	1.4	10.8	–	0.1	13.6	0.2	3.5	11.3	12.2	5.0
2 Allied medicine	1.3	1.3	9.8	1.7	5.5	25.3	19.4	14.8	35.0	36.0	23.6
3 Biological sciences	2.1	1.3	13.5	0.8	0.8	19.3	–	0.5	15.1	16.3	3.4
4 Agriculture	0.5	0.2	2.7	–	0.6	4.1	2.4	14.1	5.8	6.2	14.4
5 Physical sciences	1.6	0.5	8.9	0.5	0.5	13.6	0.1	0.6	10.3	11.1	3.2
6 Mathematical sciences	1.2	0.6	8.0	0.3	2.4	15.2	2.7	24.9	12.9	14.1	28.6
7 Engineering & technology	1.0	0.5	6.7	0.2	2.1	12.6	3.5	17.9	11.9	13.3	20.7
8 Architecture	0.8	0.8	3.8	0.6	0.6	8.7	0.8	5.2	5.1	5.9	8.8
9 Social sciences	4.2	3.4	34.1	2.9	5.1	55.7	7.6	41.8	46.3	50.9	54.2
10 Business & financial studies	2.6	5.2	22.3	2.4	17.0	93.8	68.4	245.0	105.6	110.3	296.8
11 Library & info. science	0.8	0.5	2.6	0.2	0.5	5.4	0.4	1.8	4.0	4.3	3.3
12 Languages	1.9	1.4	28.4	0.8	1.0	36.2	2.7	62.5	30.2	34.1	67.3
13 Humanities	1.0	1.3	10.8	0.5	0.3	14.3	–	2.2	11.1	12.1	4.5
14 Creative arts	1.4	0.6	19.6	0.4	6.4	29.3	36.3	95.3	61.9	63.6	97.3
15 Education[7]	8.0	7.0	18.6	3.0	2.2	47.3	2.0	37.4	26.5	30.8	55.9
16 Multi-disciplinary studies	0.7	1.0	40.5	4.0	3.7	52.1	20.6	248.3	60.9	65.6	255.4
17 GCSE, SCE and CSE	–	–	–	–	–	–	61.3	171.9	60.8	61.3	171.9
All subjects[8]	30.2	27.2	241.1	18.5	48.6	446.5	242.8	1,018.9	529.3	562.7	1,145.5

1 Excluding 84,000 (provisional) students on nursing and paramedical courses at Department of Health establishments.
2 Full-time includes sandwich, part-time comprises both day and evening.
3 Excluding data for school pupils, and for the Open University for which subject detail in this format is not available. The subject groups have been revised from the 12 groups previously used (up to 1987–8) and therefore individual subjects cannot be compared to earlier years.
4 Including courses regarded as equivalent to a first degree.
5 Including 672,000 students in all modes in England, Wales and Northern Ireland who are taking unspecified courses.
6 Including 2,128 male and 3,477 female part-time students from abroad.
7 Includes Teacher Training enrolments for universities only. Others included under the subject of study.
8 Further education totals include students in Scotland who are taking National Certificate Modules (96,000 all persons).
Source: DE (1991)

Table 4.6   Married women and lone mothers with dependent children[1]: Percentages working full-time and part-time by age of youngest dependent child, 1977–90 in Great Britain

Age of youngest dependent child and whether woman working full-time or part-time	1977–9	1979–81	1981–3	1983–5	1985–7	1987–9	1988–90
Married[2] women with dependent children							
Under 5 years							
Working full-time	5	6	6	6	9	12	13
Working part-time	22	22	19	22	25	28	30
All working[3]	27	28	25	28	34	40	43
Base = 100%	4374	4244	3838	3626	3560	3448	3227
5 years or over							
Working full-time	21	21	20	21	22	24	25
Working part-time	45	45	44	44	46	48	48
All working[3]	66	66	64	65	68	73	74
Base = 100%	7319	7148	6166	5197	5094	4789	4533
All ages							
Working full-time	15	15	14	15	17	19	20
Working part-time	37	36	35	35	37	40	41
All working[3]	52	52	49	50	54	59	61
Base = 100%	11693	11392	10004	8823	8654	8237	7760
Lone mothers							
Under 5 years							
Working full-time	13	12	7	7	9	8	8
Working part-time	13	12	11	9	11	13	12
All working[3]	26	24	18	16	20	21	20
Base = 100%	382	397	434	441	472	566	655
5 years or over							
Working full-time	26	28	25	23	23	23	25
Working part-time	29	31	29	29	32	29	30
All working[3]	56	59	54	52	55	53	56
Base = 100%	897	944	898	808	782	785	826
All ages							
Working full-time	22	23	19	17	18	17	18
Working part-time	24	25	23	22	24	23	22
All working[3]	47	49	42	39	42	40	40
Base = 100%	1279	1341	1332	1249	1254	1351	1481

1 Persons aged under 16, or aged 16–18 and in full time education, in the family unit and living in the household.

2 Including married women whose husbands were not defined as resident in the household: see Appendix A, 'Lone parent'.

3 Including a few women whose hours of work were not known, and from 1987–90 those on YTS, ET and (in 1989 only) JTS.

Source: OPCS (1990)

Table 4.7 Employment by industry: Great Britain, 1990 (000s)

	Females		Males	
	Full-time	Part-time	Full-time	Part-time
All Industries & Services	6,449.9	4,569.2	10,843.5	912.3
Agriculture, Forestry & Fishing	55.7	28.4	189.1	31.9
Energy & Water Supply	71.5	16.4	366.7	0.8
Extraction of Minerals/ Manufactured Metals	131.8	23.8	470.2	5.4
Metal Goods, Engineering, etc.	434.3	89.9	1,820.4	19.5
Other Manufacturing Industries	699.0	223.7	1,174.2	36.7
Construction	78.2	53.1	875.3	17.1
Distribution, Hotels, Catering, Repairs of which:	1,154.0	1,432.0	1,703.9	337.2
Retail Distribution	639.5	800.0	676.3	140.1
Hotels & Catering	246.2	509.6	245.5	157.4
Transport & Communication	258.9	78.6	964.4	29.2
Banking, Finance & Insurance etc. of which:	1,150.0	342.7	1,279.4	61.0
Business Services	592.5	191.6	754.3	40.8
Other Services	2,416.5	2,280.6	1,999.9	373.5

Source: EOC (1991)

labour force, there is still evidence of marked horizontal and vertical segregation. Women predominate in all service and support occupations – in clerical, catering, caring and retail spheres (see Tables 4.7 and 4.8). Where women are in manufacturing they are in unskilled and semi-skilled grades. Even educationally well qualified women tend to enter jobs like teaching and nursing, rather than entering management or scientific and technical occupations. Within each sector, the pattern is the same. Even in areas where women predominate, like teaching, nursing and social services, men hold proportionally more senior positions. Women cluster in the lower levels. This is the reality of women's lives – they are unlikely to have high status or well paid jobs even when they are relatively well qualified (see Table 4.9).

The other aspect of women's expectations and experiences is that they are likely to bear children, unless they opt not to do so or are unable to do so. Even then, the expectation is that they will. Although there have been marked changes in child bearing and child rearing patterns over the last few years, some basic constants remain. Women may now have smaller families and be likely to return to paid employment while their children are of school age but most women still take one or more breaks from paid work at some time and eventually return to work at a lower level (part-time, temporary or less well paid) than they originally left (see Table 4.10). There are three reasons for this:

- many women prefer to give full-time care to their preschool children;
- there are few adequate child care alternatives and those that do exist are costly;

Table 4.8   Employment by occupation: Great Britain, 1989

Occupational group	Females (ooos)	%	Males (ooos)	%
I Professional & related supporting management & administration	436	4.0	1,078	7.4
II Professional & related in education, welfare & health	1,551	14.1	694	4.8
III Literary, artistic and sport	151	1.4	223	1.5
IV Professional & related in science, engineering, technology & similar fields	138	1.3	846	5.8
V Management	739	6.7	2,000	13.8
VI Clerical & related	3,309	30.1	896	6.2
VII Selling	1,059	9.6	654	4.5
VIII Security & protective service	45	0.4	376	2.6
IX Catering, cleaning, hairdressing & other personal services	2,323	21.1	584	4.0
X Farming, fishing & related	79	0.7	324	2.2
XI Processing, making, repairing & related (excl. metal and electrical)	462	4.2	1,163	8.0
XII Processing, making, repairing & related (metal & electrical)	114	1.0	2,194	15.2
XIII Painting, repetitive assembling, product inspecting, packaging and related	381	3.5	542	3.7
XIV Construction and mining	*	*	888	6.1
XV Transport operating, materials moving and storing	96	0.9	1,400	9.7
XVI Miscellaneous	19	0.2	177	1.2
Inadequately described/not stated	101	0.9	435	3.0
All Persons in Employment	11,008	100.0	14,474	100.0

*Sample size too small for a reliable estimate
Source: EOC (1991)

- fathers are unlikely to be able or willing to take the main child care responsibility.

For many women breaks from paid work are both the expectation and the reality. Although there has been an increase in the number of women who take maternity leave and return full-time and an increase in the number of women with preschool children who are employed, taking time out of paid work for at least five years is the experience of most women (see Table 4.11). In recent years there has been an increase in the number of 'career break' schemes – the latest edition of the annual directory produced by the Women Returners' Network lists 44 such schemes (WRN 1992). These are mainly offered by large employers and to women who are well qualified; most women do not have this option. Many women who take time out from paid work will become 'women returners' – returners to education, training and eventually

Table 4.9 Gross weekly earnings of full-time employees[1]: By sex and type of employment, 1971–90, in Great Britain (£ and percentages)

	Males					Females				
	1971	*1981*	*1986*	*1989*	*1990*	*1971*	*1981*	*1986*	*1989*	*1990*
Manual employees										
Mean (£)	29.0	120.2	174.4	217.8	237.2	15.3	74.7	107.5	134.9	148.0
Median (£)	27.7	112.8	163.4	203.9	221.3	14.6	71.6	101.1	125.9	137.3
As percentage of median										
Highest decile	147	151	155	158	159	143	143	150	156	157
Lowest decile	68	69	65	63	63	71	70	69	69	68
Non-manual employees										
Mean (£)	38.5	160.5	244.9	323.6	354.9	20.0	97.5	145.7	195.0	215.5
Median (£)	34.0	147.0	219.4	285.7	312.1	18.2	87.7	131.5	173.5	191.8
As percentage of median										
Highest decile	175	167	175	181	182	169	172	167	174	173
Lowest decile	60	60	57	54	55	65	68	65	62	62
All employees										
Mean (£)	32.4	138.2	207.5	269.5	295.6	18.4	92.0	137.2	182.3	201.5
Median (£)	29.4	124.6	185.1	235.5	258.2	16.7	82.8	123.4	160.1	177.5
As percentage of median										
Highest decile	162	168	173	180	181	165	172	170	181	179
Lowest decile	65	64	60	59	58	66	68	65	63	63

1 Figures relate to April each year and to full-time employees on adult rates whose pay for the survey pay period was not affected by absence.
Source: CSO (1992)

employment. This is a category that has had a high profile over the last few years. It is for those women that women-only provision may be most suitable.

Although gendered experiences and structural constraints may appear to have certain effects on women, these are generalizations and different women react according to their personalities and circumstances. Of women who are likely to return to education, training or employment, there are three groups whose needs may differ considerably:

1 There are women who need to return to paid work as soon as possible, due perhaps to a change in their circumstances or because they know exactly what they want to do and have the necessary qualifications to do it.
2 There are other women who intend to return to paid employment in the near future but who have sufficient time to prepare for this – possibly to improve their qualifications or to compensate for earlier failings, or who wish to change direction.

Table 4.10 Economic activity of women: By own socio-economic group and age of youngest child, 1987–1989[1] in Great Britain (percentages)

	Professional or employer/ manager	Intermediate and junior non-manual	Skilled manual	Semi-skilled manual	Unskilled manual	All women[2] aged 16–59
Youngest child aged 0–4						
Working full-time	30	12	16	7	1	11
Working part-time	27	27	34	22	46	26
Unemployed	3	6	5	6	6	6
Economically inactive	39	54	45	64	47	57
Youngest child aged 5–9						
Working full-time	37	19	27	11	1	17
Working part-time	39	48	43	48	76	48
Unemployed	2	4	3	5	4	4
Economically inactive	21	29	26	36	20	31
Youngest child aged 10 and over						
Working full-time	61	32	36	21	7	30
Working part-time	26	45	39	47	65	44
Unemployed	2	2	2	5	3	3
Economically inactive	11	21	22	27	25	23
No dependent children						
Working full-time	77	62	52	40	9	50
Working part-time	9	18	19	26	56	22
Unemployed	2	3	4	7	4	5
Economically inactive	11	15	24	25	31	22
All women aged 16–59						
Working full-time	65	44	39	27	7	36
Working part-time	16	27	28	31	59	28
Unemployed	2	4	4	6	4	5
Economically inactive	16	24	28	34	31	30

1 Combined data.
2 Includes women in the armed forces, inadequately described occupations and those who have never worked.
Source: CSO (1992)

Table 4.11 Lone mothers and married women with dependent children[1]: Percentage working full-time and part-time by age of youngest dependent child and marital status in Great Britain, 1988–90 combined

Age of youngest dependent child and whether woman working full-time or part-time	Lone mothers					Married[2] women with dependent children
	Single	Widowed	Divorced	Separated	All lone mothers	
Under 5 years						
Working full-time	9	[12]	6	7	8	13
Working part-time	9	[38]	18	13	12	30
All working[3]	19	[50]	24	20	20	43
Base = 100%	370	8	131	146	655	3229
Over 5 years:						
Working full-time	21	25	27	25	26	25
Working part-time	28	33	29	32	30	48
All working[3]	49	58	58	58	56	74
Base = 100%	130	93	433	175	831	4534
All ages:						
Working full-time	12	24	23	17	18	20
Working part-time	14	34	26	23	22	41
All working[3]	27	57	50	40	41	61
Base = 100%	500	101	564	321	1486	7763

1 Dependent children are persons aged under 16, or aged 16–18 and in full-time education, in the family unit, and living in the household.
2 Including married women whose husbands were not defined as resident in the household.
3 'All working' includes those on Government Schemes and those whose hours of work were not known.
Source: OPCS (1990)

3 There are women who intend to continue in their full-time domestic role, probably with caring responsibilities, who need the stimulus or challenge of education and would benefit from a shared supportive experience. These may be women who have qualifications, who feel they need to be stretched and challenged; they may be women with no qualifications, for whom education may not seem initially appropriate.

Depending on their circumstances, the actual provision appropriate for women in these three groups may vary but they are likely to have certain things in common:

- they will need information, advice and guidance about what is available and most appropriate for them;
- they will need practical arrangements that suit their other responsibilities, especially if they are carers;
- they need resources that recognize the possible limitations of their financial situation, whether they are on benefits or dependent on a male partner.

Educational opportunities for adults as a whole and for women in particular are varied and unevenly distributed, provided by a range of institutions and organizations. Many women will have incomplete knowledge of what is available. Many women's knowledge of what is appropriate will be even more limited unless they have access to a good educational guidance service for adults in their area or discover a course which incorporates personal advice and counselling.

The requirements of women who have the care of preschool or school-age children, or elderly dependants will vary. The timing and location of provision is as important as the adequate provision of child care, and other needs have to be recognized. Relatively few unwaged women (i.e. women not in paid employment) have unrestricted access to their own financial resources. Many women in part-time, temporary or low paid work have no spare money. Both of these requirements must be recognized by those who provide educational opportunities for women. Most important of all is that they recognize the particular experiences of women due to the expectations and demands of our gendered society.

For women who have spent some years in full-time domestic responsibilities and caring for children, it is not simply a matter of having information about the options that are available or advice and guidance about what would be most appropriate. Nor is it only a matter of organizing the practicalities, although that in itself can be difficult enough. As the discussion of the WEA provision in the previous chapter emphasized, providers of women's education may need to help women cope with change.

Women are socialized in preparation for their role as wife and mother. Society expects women to fulfil this role unselfishly – to deny their own wishes in deference to those of the family. One of the effects of full-time motherhood in our society is that women can lose a sense of their own identity because they have become used to suppressing their own needs in preference to those of others. They are not used to making demands for themselves and may feel guilty if they allow their own needs or desires to take precedence over those of the rest of the family.

Society devalues motherhood, paying lip service to its importance in rhetoric about the significance of 'family values' – values which are presumed to be the responsibility of the wife and mother. To seek education or training, even to contemplate a return to employment unless it is financially necessary, for some women is seen as neglecting the family and pursuing their own selfish ends. If that education or training costs money, it is even more likely to be unacceptable. The feeling of guilt never leaves a woman who reduces her domestic commitment by re-entering education or training or returning to paid work. It resurges to the fore every time a child is ill or there is a clash of commitments. The family takes priority but at a cost – the dual role makes demands that many women find unbearable, feelings of guilt making them over-compensate for their implied neglect.

The devaluing of women and the subordination of their needs to those of the family may cause women to lose confidence – confidence in their ability to cope with anything other than being a good wife and mother, confidence to achieve in education or to cope with a dual career. Images of 'superwomen' and articles on how to manage home and work do not help because any failure to live up to that ideal reinforces the feelings of inadequacy. The domestic role receives no reward and no recognition. Most women do not realize that the skills of successfully running a home and family are many and diverse and that most of those skills are transferable to other settings.

Entering a women-only group as the first step back into education or training prior to a return to employment, and discovering that other women share this sense of guilt and feeling of inadequacy helps women to realize that their feelings do not represent a deficiency in themselves but are a consequence of the expectations of society as a whole. Regaining confidence, through achieving in a supportive environment of being helped to recognize their skills and strengths, helps to enhance self-respect and self-confidence.

In mixed groups, the specific experiences of women as women and their particular feelings may not be shared. Men are socialized in different ways and many do not realize how inhibiting their presence can be for women who are just regaining confidence. It may not seem appropriate for women to share their concerns with men. Space is needed for women's concerns and perceptions to be shared and supported.

These are the prime requirements of educational provision for many women at the point of re-entry – a transitional experience while they rediscover old skills and gain new ones. Above all, they need a space where the changes within themselves, and possibly in their circumstances, can be experienced in a supportive environment.

Other arguments for women-only provision

Most women-only provision in education and training can be seen as transitional, providing opportunities for women who are intending to enter or re-enter the work force, or provision for unwaged women making their first step back to education or training after a period of full-time domestic responsibility. Many women have to make this transition at one or more points in their lives. As well as the arguments outlined above, there seem to be several other reasons why even quite capable and well-qualified women find re-entry difficult.

The longer women spend out of paid work the less confident they are about returning. Not only have technological, economic and social changes left them feeling outdated but habits and routines of the domestic sphere, demanding as they are, are seen as inappropriate for the outside world. Many women feel that they did not fulfil their potential at school or were forced ill-advisedly into jobs they did not really want. Some have few or inappropriate qualifications. Not wanting to return to the same job as before stops many women from working at all because they have no idea what else they can or want to do.

There is widespread ambivalence in our society about the roles of women. On the one hand, women are recognized as a wasted resource and as potentially skilled and able workers. On the other hand, there is a strong expectation that they should take full responsibility for all domestic and caring tasks. This dual role appears to pose problems for employers who are worried that women will place greater emphasis on their domestic role and therefore prove 'unreliable' workers. For women the tension between the roles is very real. Trying to cope with two or more conflicting demands enhances feelings of guilt and stress. This is not helped by a society which takes no responsibility for child care whilst parents are engaged in other activities.

Many women get considerable satisfaction from their domestic role, particularly while their children are small and more time consuming, but they reach a critical point when their youngest child starts school. Although the responsibility for child care does not disappear at this point, the daily duties do change. As children get older and independence is reached, many women who have devoted themselves to domestic duties and child care are faced with a problem. It is not unusual for such women to feel useless and unwanted even though they may have many potentially productive years ahead of them.

Changing standards and expectations about marriage and family life leave many women facing unforeseen disruption and change in their lives. Events such as unemployment, divorce and death place unexpected demands on them. Such is the 'myth' of the contented nuclear family – male breadwinner, dependent wife, two children and dog – that many women do not anticipate disruptive events and do not prepare for them.

There is a lot of evidence to suggest that we live in a male dominated society, where power and control lies in the hands of men and decisions are taken by them. In mixed groupings, men tend to dominate, not necessarily by design but through custom. Women are less likely to challenge male assumptions in mixed company and are not given space to explore their own perspectives. Certain topics are taboo in mixed discussion groups and yet are of great importance to women. Despite the changes of the past few years and some moves towards equality, there are still large areas of work and activity where few women feel confident – in so-called non-traditional and manual trades, in management, in science and technology, for example. If women are to enter these arenas, they must have opportunities to acquire the skills and knowledge they need without the inhibition of competing with men.

The different experiences of women and men, both during initial schooling and in the world of work, mean that many women lack confidence in their ability to learn. Traditional approaches to learning are individualized and competitive, rewarding the most successful and punishing or ignoring those who fail. It is not surprising that women are fearful about re-entering an educational setting.

These considerations reinforce the need for women-only provision at the point of re-entry and for certain subjects. Not only do women need the practical support to enable them to cope with the demands of their dual role, but they also need the emotional support through the re-entry experience.

One of the few advantages of the broken work pattern of women's lives is that it does provide an opportunity to reassess, to rethink what they want to do and to prepare for it. Educational experiences in themselves can be a powerful force for change. Women who re-enter often find themselves changing in ways that they had not anticipated and this has implications both for the providers of the educational experience and for those with whom the woman lives. The providers of women-only courses are in a unique position to offer support to their women students and most are skilled in giving this support. It is clear that the support of the other students in the group is also important.

It is possible to argue that women-only provision has been shown to be effective in empowering women and preparing them for further education, training or work. Experience has given us some idea of what women need during this period of reorientation and what changes are likely to occur. Of all the current theories of adult learning, there are two which contribute a great deal to our understanding of what happens on women-only courses and which support the case for women-only provision. One is the book by Belenky *et al.* (1986) and the other is the work of Mezirow (1981) on 'perspective transformation'.

Belenky and her colleagues draw on interview material from a wide range of women learners and argue that most formal education is not appropriate for women. Women feel alienated in academic settings; they feel unheard even when they have something important to say. Even when the content of the learning experience is relevant to women, teaching and evaluation methods are not compatible with women's preferred styles of learning. Most learning is shaped by male culture; women's thinking styles, which may be more emotional, intuitive or personalized, are devalued.

Belenky *et al.* go on to explore 'women's ways of knowing', using five categories:

- silence
- received knowledge

- subjective knowledge
- procedural knowledge
- constructed knowledge.

Within their descriptions of each category there are examples which demonstrate the importance of women-only groups. For example, Belenky *et al.* (1986) analyse procedural knowledge as separate or connected. In connected knowing, the importance of the commonality of the group is demonstrated.

> People could criticize each other's work in class and accept each other's criticism because members of the group shared a similar experience. This is the only source of expertise connected knowers recognize, the only sort of criticism they easily accept. Authority in connected knowing rests not on power or status or certification but on commonality of experience.

The importance of realistic confidence building is emphasized and needed right from the start of the learning experience.

> A woman, like any other human being, does need to know that the mind makes mistakes; but our interviews have convinced us that every woman, regardless of age, social class, ethnicity, and academic achievement, needs to know that she is capable of intelligent thought, and she needs to know it right away.

Belenky *et al.* (1986) conclude:

> We have argued in this book that educators can help women develop their own authentic voices if they emphasize connection over separation, understanding and acceptance over assessment, and collaboration over debate; if they accord respect to and allow time for the knowledge that emerges from firsthand experience; if instead of imposing their own expectations and arbitrary requirements, they encourage students to evolve their own patterns of work based on the problems they are pursuing. These are the lessons we have learned in listening to women's voices.

These are also the lessons that have been learned from many examples of women-only provision. Although Belenky and her colleagues do not argue for a developmental progression in women's ways of knowing, they do recognize the importance of change. The process of change that can occur through women's education is the theme of work by Mezirow, which came from his studies of women re-entrants.

Mezirow argues that through learning experiences adults can engage in reflective thinking which leads to a transformation in our 'frameworks of reference'. These are the meaning schemes and meaning perspectives which inform our actions and with which we make sense of our experiences. He describes a series of changes which may occur when an individual is challenged by a 'disorientating dilemma' which may be caused by an event (e.g. a divorce) or by a significant encounter (e.g. through art or literature). The ten elements he outlines are:

1. a disorientating dilemma;
2. self-examination;
3. a critical assessment of internalized role assumptions and a sense of alienation from traditional social expectations;
4. relating one's discontent to similar experiences of others or to public issues – recognizing that one's problem is shared and not exclusively a private matter;
5. exploring options for new ways of acting;
6. building competence and self-knowledge in new roles;
7. planning a course of action;
8. acquiring knowledge and skills for implementing one's plans;
9. provisional efforts to try new roles and to assess feedback;
10. a reintegration into society on the basis of conditions dictated by the new perspective.

(Mezirow 1981)

It can be seen how women re-entering an educational experience because of, or confronted by, a disorientation can progress through these changes. The 'disorientating dilemma' may be an event prior to a woman starting a course (e.g. her youngest child starting school; divorce or separation) or during a course (e.g. through a discussion of women's roles; an examination of women in literature etc.). The course content often encourages women to explore themselves – their past histories, their current situations and their future options. Linked to an exploration of women's roles in society which locates their experience in a wider context, many women come to have a new perspective on themselves.

The fourth element in Mezirow's process is particularly significant for women's education and to the approach of the WLM as a whole. Recognizing that a personal problem is shared and that the causes of that problem and the associated feelings of guilt or inadequacy are also shared can be an important step in coming to terms with it. This sense of commonality is one of the main strengths of women-only provision.

Most women's education explores the fifth, sixth and seventh elements of his analysis, encouraging women to move on to the eighth element. Women should leave a course aware of what options are available and how to gain the necessary skills to take up a future option, even if they choose not to do so at that particular time. Some provision allows for the ninth element, encouraging women to confront change while still in the supportive care of the group. This may involve change in personal relationships or trying out entry to the public arena – through taster courses, work experience or shadowing roles.

Element ten in Mezirow's outline appears to suggest that the disorientation is solved and successful reintegration occurs. For many women this may take some time. It also suggests that the desired aim is reintegration into existing society – and for many women that may be so. However, for some, one of the aims of women's education is to raise awareness of the social constraints on women and to empower them to challenge this. Mezirow's analysis makes no provision for this new awareness and confrontation. The main task for women would be to challenge male dominance and patriarchal structures, in both private and public arenas.

The implications for tutors of women-only courses is that they should be capable of initiating or facilitating such change and supporting it. Another implication concerns the support of the student group. If what is involved is a potential change in a 'framework of reference', the extent to which others share that new framework may make it more acceptable. Such examples are well known to those who work with women in this way. When we talk of empowering women to make their own decisions, to move forward, to challenge assumptions, we are equipping them to come to terms with new frameworks.

This is not to assume that all women want or need to make changes, either in themselves or in their circumstances, nor to assume that this transformation can only occur in a women-only context. What I am arguing is that the content and methods of women-only provision are designed with this challenging in mind.

In recent years there have been numerous detailed accounts of provision for women only and many examples of good practice. There has, however, been little detailed research of what exactly is involved in this 'good practice' and what it is that really makes the experience so important for the women concerned. Although there have been several attempts to describe the curriculum, there have been few attempts to analyse it. In 1987 the Further Education Unit funded a long-term research project into the curriculum of women-only provision (Coats *et al.* 1988). This research set out to examine in depth six different examples of such provision, in an attempt to discover what curriculum is needed and how it should be best delivered if the needs of women are to be met. This task is of critical importance if we are to continue to develop good women's education and if the lessons learned from women-only provision are to be transferred to other areas of mixed provision and embedded in mainstream further and higher education. Before looking at the curriculum in more detail, however, it is useful to summarize the kind of women-only provision we are arguing is appropriate.

Types of women-only provision

In the introductory chapter of this book, I quoted from the SDA which outlines the various criteria under which single gender provision can be made. Over the last 20 years the kinds of provision, both in education and training, which have recognized these criteria have taken different forms and been organized by a whole range of providers. As can be seen from Table 4.12, the categories include:

Table 4.12 Definitions and descriptions of educational opportunities for women in England and Wales

	Objectives	Target group	Level	Content
Women into science, technology and engineering	Courses to encourage women to return to or enter science, technology or engineering. Some courses offer a 'conversion' route for those with non-scientific qualifications. Provides access to degree courses or less advanced courses (BTEC Ordinary and Higher Diplomas) in science, technology or engineering. May lead to jobs at technician level.	Women only, especially women returners with a scientific background.	Courses may require a Maths or Science GCE O or A level or some evidence of study or experience in a scientific subject. Many pre-degree courses act as an access route to HE.	Maths and science subjects – physics, chemistry, computing etc.
Advancement courses for women	To encourage women to aim for supervisory or management positions. Most popular qualification is certification by National Examinations Board for Supervisory Management (NEBSM).	Women who have previously held supervisory positions or who demonstrate potential to do so.	Many at pre-degree level but some post-graduate courses.	Managerial skills; personal development; advice and guidance; usually some information technology.
Women-only non-traditional (male) skill areas	To provide opportunity for women to experience non-traditional areas of work; to gain basic skills training in them, without being intimidated by competition with men. To encourage women to enter occupations previously dominated by men. Leads to further courses in chosen skill area in colleges of further education, or employment.	All courses are women-only. All women are welcomed, especially those with few or no qualifications. Some provision aims to attract black women.	Most provision is at basic level, working towards City and Guilds modules.	Training in specific skill areas such as electronics, computing, plumbing, carpentry, painting and decorating, motor vehicle mechanics. Includes personal development and confidence-building; job-seeking skills and self-employment advice.

Table 4.12 (Cont'd)

	Objectives	Target group	Level	Content
Reorientation and bridging programmes; women returner courses	Re-entry courses for women wanting to return to education, training or employment after a period of full-time domestic and family responsibility. Premise underlying reorientation courses is that each individual woman makes an informed choice about her own future, therefore courses have several possible outcomes – education and training courses; employment or self-employment; voluntary work or continued domestic responsibilities.	Unwaged women; both those looking to return to work and those wanting to explore possible options for the future. Some programmes target specific groups of women – e.g. those with few or no educational qualifications; those living in a particular locality.	Courses usually non-academic and non-certified, catering for the needs of any unwaged woman.	Confidence-building, individual and group counselling, advice and guidance and career planning are the main components; plus women's studies or specific subject areas (psychology, sociology, literature etc.). Some incorporate basic learning skills.
Women's studies programmes	Courses which make visible the experiences of women in any discipline or subject area or attempt to locate that experience in a wider social and political context. Currently one full degree course (BA) in women's studies and several MA programmes in universities and polytechnics. Women's studies modules may form part of courses for social workers and teachers, as well as degree options.	All women.	Women's studies programmes provided at all levels from non-certified short courses to degree (BA) and post-graduate (MA) level.	Depends on the level and interests of the students but areas covered are likely to be topics such as Women in History, Women in Health, Women in Literature etc.

Access to higher education courses	To provide alternative route for adults to enter higher education; avoids need to gain GCE Advanced Levels. Many courses linked with an assured interview or entry to degree course for successful completion.	Some access courses for women only, most mixed; some target specific groups – e.g. black people or working-class people.	Pre-degree level. Most accept students with no educational qualifications but look for high motivation and potential for serious study.	Main subject are a plus learning skills; personal counselling and educational guidance.
Vocational and pre-vocational programmes	To provide vocational training for whole range of potential careers. In theory, women may apply for all vocational areas but have tended to cluster in clerical work and in service industries (catering, caring, hairdressing etc.). Courses may lead to BTEC, RSA, City and Guilds qualifications.	Provision for unwaged women covers both initial training and updating. Courses for women returners usually aimed at those with some prior experience in the field.	Provision at all levels, from complete beginners to those updating their skills. Courses which demand entrance qualifications (e.g. 4 GCSE passes) may waive them for mature students.	Syllabus as laid down by examining body in specific subject. Courses targeted at women returners may include confidence-building and counselling; advice and guidance sessions.

Source: Replan (1991b)

- Positive action programmes: for entry to non-traditional areas (e.g. Women into Electronics); for promotion in specific roles (e.g. Women into Management);
- Updating for women returners: professional updating (e.g. for teachers, doctors etc.); updating skills (e.g. word processing and new office skills);
- Reorientation courses: New Opportunities for Women and Wider Opportunities for Women (Wider Horizons, Fresh Start etc.);
- Informal, community based groups: encouraging women out of the home (e.g. Out of the House); building on school or preschool groups;
- Return to study: second chance courses for women; pre-access courses for women.

This provision will be examined in more detail in the following chapters.

5 The Characteristics of Good Women-only Provision

There have been several attempts to describe or prescribe the important characteristics of women-only provision and to argue for improved resourcing which recognizes its particular requirements. A very useful practical checklist was compiled by participants at a Replan Conference in the West Midlands in 1991 (Replan 1991a). Although not specifically designed for women-only work, it covered the practicalities involved in making good provision for women. A previous Replan conference on educational provision for 'women returners' had indicated that there was a need for some guidelines for those who wanted to provide good educational experiences for women – in the community, in colleges, or through various organizations and agencies. Subsequently, participants and others were invited to attend a follow-up event at which the checklist was discussed and designed.

The list was compiled to be as wide ranging as possible, so that some items applied only to institutions like colleges; more community based work might have found some items were not relevant for them. For convenience, the checklist referred to 'courses', 'students' and 'tutors' throughout, although it was recognized that not all provision used these more formal terms. The checklist was divided into four sections:

- before entry
- on entry
- during provision
- moving on.

It was envisaged that providers would work through the whole checklist before planning or starting any provision for women and might return to it at any stage. It would have been particularly appropriate to work through the list again during any review stage at the end of the provision or make use of the list in staff development sessions.

Checklist for good practice for educational provision for women: before entry

Developing and designing the course

Are you clear why you are offering this course? Have you agreed aims for the course? Have you decided on the student target group? For which women is the course designed? Is the provision based on a thorough knowledge of the local community?

Assessing the local labour market

Have you assessed the needs of the local labour market? Have you asked employers what they want? Are there skill shortages in your area? Will there be jobs for the women who complete your course if that is what they want?

Funding

Have you costed the provision fully? Have you got adequate funding for this course? What exactly does the funding cover? Have you explored all the possibilities for additional funding? Is your funding secure? Have you checked the criteria and used the correct wording in any funding application? Is funding ongoing or does it require renewal? Have you considered shared funding with another institution, agency, organization or employer? Does your funding dictate what students you accept? Does your funding place restrictions on what you can provide? Does your funding impose evaluation criteria?

Deciding on the venue

Is the venue suitable, accessible and friendly? Is the atmosphere of the venue appropriate for mature women students? Have you looked at alternative venues? Have you considered taking the provision out into the community? Have you considered all the options for a venue in the community? Can you move resources/equipment out into the community? Is it appropriate to start in the community and later move the provision into the college?

Outreach

Who is responsible for outreach? Have you allowed sufficient time for outreach? Is it timetabled if necessary? Have you considered paying someone in the community to help with outreach? Do you have contacts in the community with whom you can work?

Publicity

Have you considered carefully the name of the course? Have you designed different kinds of publicity material? Have you looked carefully at any graphics? Does the material contain all the essential information? Does it make clear for whom the course is designed? Have you thought of including success stories and comments from previous (real) students? Have you considered carefully where publicity material will be distributed? Are you using local networks to distribute your publicity? Do all the local advice agencies know about your provision? Have you got anyone (staff or students) prepared to give talks about the provision? Are you using other means of publicity such as local radio, local free papers etc.? Is it appropriate to use a local celebrity in your publicity? Have you considered holding 'open days' specifically for women? Have you fully marketed your course both internally and externally?

Links with other providers and agencies

Have you built up links with other institutions, organizations and support agencies? Have you developed a network for referral? Do you know what else is provided for women in your locality? Are there any appropriate 'feeder' courses in your locality? Have you made links with them?

Information, advice and guidance for students

Do you provide a central information and referral service for students? Is it fully informed about the needs of mature women students? Can the prospective student get full details about the course? Is the first point of contact clear and sympathetic to the needs of women? Is there a named contact and telephone number that women can contact for information and advice? Can they be helped to decide if this provision is appropriate for them? Are all the details about the course such as hours per week and weeks per year etc., clear? Is it clear how much home study is required? Have you made it clear if there are there any residentials involved? Do students understand if work experience is part of the course? What starting qualifications are needed? Is Accreditation of Prior Learning (APL) appropriate and suited to the students? Are taster courses available? Is there advice on preparing for a course?

Fees

Can women get accurate and confidential advice about fees? Are concessions available and is this made clear to all enquirers? Who qualifies for concessions? Is there help for women who are dependent on working partners? Have you checked that there are no additional expenses and if there are, is this made clear to prospective students?

Staffing the course

Have you been able to recruit suitable staff? Will they act as realistic role models for the women students? Have all the staff involved in the course had appropriate training? Is it possible to have cotutoring or double staffing? Are all the staff committed to the aims of the course? Have your reception and telephone staff been appropriately trained?

On entry

On arrival

Is there a welcome for new students? Is it clearly signposted where to go? Do students know who to see when they get there? Is there someone to meet them? What arrangements have been made for induction? Are students introduced to all the staff concerned with their course? Is there a college booklet for mature students or for women students? Is there a course booklet for students which makes clear exactly what they may expect? Is it clear if there is a Mature Students Union? Is it made clear if there is a women's officer? What equal opportunities policy and practice exists and are students made aware of this? Do students know where to go for assistance if they meet racist, sexist or ageist attitudes and practice?

Support for individual students

Does every student have a personal tutor or individual contact person? What counselling service is available for individual students? Do students know who to turn to if an unexpected emergency arises? Are there opportunities for students to check if they are on the right course and at the right level? Can they change course if necessary? Is learning skills support available? Is there a drop-in workshop? Is language support available as required? Is there a confidence building component to every course?

Practical arrangements

Is the provision always in the same room(s) and not moved around? Is there a 'base' room for students on the course? Is there a common room for mature students? Are the library opening times convenient for women? Is there adequate parking for staff and students? Is the venue on a bus route or could buses be asked to stop there? Are the timings of sessions convenient for women who have other responsibilities (i.e. within school hours and within school terms)? Is there help for women who have dependent relatives? What child care provision is available? Is it of high quality with good equipment and trained staff? Is child care free or are the charges reasonable? Is there access and storage for prams and pushchairs? Can children be cared for at lunch time or do parents have to look after them? Are children allowed in the canteen and is appropriate food available? Are the toilet facilities adequate for both women and children? Are there changing rooms for women, if necessary, and for babies? Is there good access for women with disabilities? Is there adequate lighting both inside and outside the college? Are there adequate security patrols?

During provision

Continuous assessment and monitoring

Do you have a structured way of checking that everything is going well on the course? Are you checking that the needs of particular groups of women are being met (e.g. black women, older women, women with disabilities)? How are you keeping records of progress for each student? If there is continuous assessment of the students, how are you monitoring this? Are students being encouraged to assess their own needs and to reflect on the progress they are making? How can students give you ongoing feedback on their experiences on the course? Have you built in time for advice and guidance throughout the course so that future options are addressed?

Curriculum and methodology

Can the curriculum be negotiated and how is this being done? Have you checked that learning is cooperative not competitive? Have you checked the group dynamics? Are there any problems? Are you monitoring the effects of the group and using this to support the students? Are the demands of the course increasing as appropriate? How much flexibility can be built into the course and how is this handled? Are you encouraging students to develop independence and to prepare for moving on at the end of the course?

Particular concerns

If there are residential courses, what happens to those who cannot attend? What support is there for students on their work placements? Can you arrange a 'mop up' time for students when they can catch up on things they have missed or found difficult?

Staff support

Are the staff consistent, supportive, sympathetic and responsible? Is there ongoing support for all the tutors on the course? Have you checked that all staff understand the other demands faced by students on the course? Are staff development needs being assessed and provided for?

Moving on

Assessment and accreditation

Does the college offer its own certification? Have you made clear the value of any certificates? What provision have you made for students who 'fail'?

Information, guidance and counselling

Are students aware of all the possible progression routes? Have you mapped all the options? Have you got information on what other providers can offer? Was there adequate time in the course to cover this? What can you provide for students who may not want to move on? Have you encouraged students to set up self-help groups for when the course finishes?

Monitoring and evaluation

Who is going to do the evaluation and to whom will the results be made available? Have you made arrangements to follow up and evaluate the destinations of the students? Have you checked the drop out rate and what system do you have for coping with this? Are the fees returnable for students who for good reason cannot complete the course?

Review and further development

What changes can and will be made in the provision after monitoring and evaluation? Are you aware of the need for more staff development and who will provide this? Who will look at the need for more curriculum development?

Conclusion

Why are you using this checklist? What will you do with the results? Will you come back to it at the end of the course? Should you be making any changes/additions that are relevant to your provision?

Support for women learners: requirements and resources

The argument of this section is that institutions and organizations which want to attract and provide for women students, educating women in a way that is relevant to women, need to note the specific requirements of women who want to return to or continue in education. Those requirements may involve extra resources for women (Coats 1989b).

Although there may be more women than men involved in adult education, it is important to ask which women are involved and to recognize the needs of all women, including working-class women, unwaged women, women with young children, black women, lesbian women, rural women, older women and women with disabilities. It cannot be assumed that any provision for women will automatically attract all women or meet the specific needs of various groups of women. In particular, it means going out to women who do not see that education is relevant for them or women who have been damaged by earlier educational experiences.

There are three components to attracting women – outreach, publicity and information, advice and guidance. Outreach involves going out to women where they are, finding out what they need. It takes time and resources; it is best done by skilled local women who are known in the community.

Publicity has to show that the provision is relevant to women and appropriate for particular women; it needs to specify that, for example, working-class women or women without educational qualifications are welcome. Face-to-face outreach and publicity is more effective than leaflets, local papers and local radio – although all these should be used too. Giving a named person to contact may encourage women to make enquiries and those responding to enquirers must be informed and ready to help.

Women need information, advice and guidance; they need to know what is available and appropriate for them. No course should recruit a woman without discerning if it is what she needs. Information, advice and guidance should be available before, during and at the end of a course; it should be local, informed and realistic.

Supporting women learners means recognizing that they will have specific needs and making resources available to meet those needs. The basic needs of women returning to or continuing in education are:

- accessibility – in terms of time and place
- provision for the care of dependants
- counselling and support for women students.

Women need daily and weekly timetables which allow for their other responsibilities and which recognize the length of the school day, half terms and holidays. Accessibility means holding classes in a place that is welcoming and signposted, where reception staff are helpful and informed. It means using a place that is local or where transport is convenient or provided, and above all, a place where women, whatever their disability or disposition, can gain access and feel comfortable. Women need a secure space in which to store possessions and to have refreshments and meals, to relax and to work. In shared accommodation – a student refectory for example – which is dominated by younger people, mature students and particularly women, should be treated as though they have a right to be there.

Although the battle for adequate child care provision has not been won, there is a greater awareness that students who are parents need some facility provided. Limited crèche places or a playgroup are not sufficient, however. Either provision or finance for babies, for preschool children and, for school age children when necessary, are required. There has been increasing concern about the quality of the provision and the terms and conditions of the (usually) women who work there, plus a realization that many women prefer to leave their children in a familiar environment – with their own playgroup or child minder – and so need financial help instead. This is even more true for the many women who now have responsibility for other dependants – elderly parents, sick or disabled relatives. One estimate suggests that more women look after other dependants than look after preschool children. If the education needs of these women are to be met, then imaginative and innovative schemes must be devised and resourced – funding for respite care for example.

Most educational provision designed for women only provides ongoing individual and group counselling and support, but women who progress to mainstream provision are often left isolated and unsupported. Even worse, the support that is offered, through a personal tutor for example, although well-meaning, can be entirely inappropriate. The needs of a black, working-class woman with domestic responsibilities are not the same as those of a white middle-class, rugby-playing adolescent male.

If the requirements and resourcing of women students are recognized, so too must be those of the staff, especially their conditions of service and need for support. Many women tutors in both voluntary and statutory sector educational provision for adults are part-timers, lacking time and resources for preparation; not offered staff development or training; on temporary or indefinite contracts; and working in isolation and inadequate conditions. If adult education generally is underresourced and poorly equipped, women's education is even more so. Draughty church halls or school desks for daytime classes, boxes of books in the corner, and crèches where all the toys have to be unpacked and repacked each session are common.

Of all the barriers which make education unavailable to many women, finance is probably the greatest. Not only is the cost of course fees, crèche fees and bus fares a prohibitive barrier, but serious study has other costs – books and stationery, visits and other events. Women on benefits or dependent on a claimant partner are able to get reduced fees in some organizations and authorities, but the pattern is uneven. Dependent women who have no access to spare money or those with low-paid partners are often in difficulty and do not qualify for reductions. Even women who are able to get mandatory or discretionary grants are not exempt from problems. Not only are these funds inadequate but they are often delayed. Women with dependants find they cannot claim for them during the long holidays (and sometimes have not been told this in advance); women whose marriages ended years before are told to get maintenance from exhusbands; and some authorities require a husband to sign a form giving permission for his wife to study before a grant is given. These are some of the barriers which women face as they return or continue to study.

The curriculum requirements of women have less to do with resourcing and are more a matter of recognition – of how both content and methodology can be made relevant to women. Deciding what is to be offered to women means looking further than women's interests and issues – the reinforcements of stereotypical domestic skills or the emphasis on appearance – and finding relevance for women in everything that is offered. It may mean, too, deliberately compensating for women's absence in some areas, in what are commonly called 'non-traditional' skills or scientific subjects, by providing women-only sessions, groupings or courses.

It is important to recognize women's needs in deciding how the content shall be delivered. Many women prefer cooperative and shared learning, active participation rather than passive reception, drawing on and valuing their own experiences, relating new knowledge to prior learning, recognizing affective as well as cognitive components of learning.

The need for personal counselling and support has already been mentioned. Personal learning support is needed too – back-up provision in language, literacy, numeracy and study skills. Support may also mean providing adequate time and space for private study away from the consistent demands of family, or understanding that most women's lives do not follow an even course or regular pattern but are fragmented and inconsistent, with unforeseen emergencies. Thus flexibility – not concessionary or favoured but realistic – is required.

This discussion of the characteristics of women's education and the basic requirements and resources for good provision has focused mainly on the practicalities and the planning. There are numerous other guidelines and checklists available which address these issues in some detail. There is far less material, however, on the actual curriculum of women's education.

The curriculum of women's education

This section draws heavily on two particular sources:

1. a paper on the curriculum of women-only education, presented at the 'Women Educating Women' conference, organized in London by the Open University and the National Extension College in September 1989 (Coats 1989a).
2. a paper by Gisela Pravda, presented at the OU/ICDE conference, 'The

Student, Community and Curriculum' in Cambridge in September 1991
(Pravda 1991).

Women-only provision needs a women-centred curriculum

The first paper (Coats 1989a) looked at some of the characteristics of 'women-centred' provision and drew on ideas from both feminist and radical education. It argued that it is not enough to make the case for women-only education; it is important also to define more clearly the characteristics of it. To do this effectively we need to focus on the experiences of the women who are at the centre of the process of what might be called a 'women-centred curriculum'.

It is necessary to consider the whole curriculum and not just the content of what is provided or the methodology of how it is taught, but to look also at the values and ideologies which inform its design, the structures within which it is delivered, the evaluation and development which redefines and redesigns its ongoing practice. The paper was an attempt to analyse and model a 'women-centred' curriculum.

Formal curriculum theory is not particularly helpful to an analysis of women-centred provision although there have been several very useful attempts to define and describe the essential characteristics of women's education. The technique used here was to list what seem to be the main characteristics and to try to 'cluster' them as seemed appropriate. Six clusters were presented, but there could have been others or some could have been merged. There was overlap and repetition – as indeed there is in practice.

A women-centred curriculum . . .
. . . Uses subjective experience and affective processes:

- respects the individuality of women;
- starts from the experiences of women;
- recognizes the subjective response and values it;
- acknowledges affective as well as cognitive processes;
- says it's OK to explore yourself and your feelings;
- gives space for each woman to explore her thoughts and feelings;
- enhances confidence in skills/knowledge/abilities already possessed;
- uses anecdotes and examples from women's lived experiences.

. . . Locates gendered experience in a wider social context:

- recognizes and values the distinctive attributes of women;
- acknowledges the value of the domestic role;
- analyses the mechanisms and manifestations of oppression;
- deconstructs the gendered experience of initial schooling;
- focuses the content on women's experiences;

- uses examples/illustrations that are relevant to women;
- shows that 'the personal is the political'.

. . . Recognizes the importance of group support and collective action:

- supports women who are experiencing personal change;
- encourages and values the contribution of each woman;
- does not expose any woman against her will;
- develops collectivity and support structures;
- creates a 'safe' environment which does not threaten;
- sets any challenge only when there is support to help meet it;
- allows women to discover that their problems are shared;
- allows women to discover that their feelings are shared;
- creates a shared learning environment in which students and tutors all contribute.

. . . Uses methods and strategies that encourage participation:

- asks open rather than closed questions;
- reduces the risk of damage from 'wrong' answers;
- encourages all women to participate actively;
- makes it possible to say 'I do not understand';
- provides experience in solving problems and finding solutions;
- allows for experiential learning and reflectivity;
- gives opportunities for creative expression;
- focuses on perceived, not received, knowledge;
- fosters cooperation, not competition;
- relates all learning to experience;
- helps women to identify and develop their own learning skills;
- makes new ways of learning exciting and enjoyable.

. . . Continuously reviews, evaluates and develops:

- provides a student controlled or negotiated curriculum;
- encourages continuous and honest feedback;
- leads to the empowerment of individual women and the group;
- devises strategies for continued learning;
- allows for progression by providing information and guidance;
- prepares women for moving on by developing transitional skills.

. . . Removes barriers and improves practicalities:

- makes sure that timing, cost and place are appropriate;
- maximizes accessibility;
- provides facilities or resources for the care of dependants;
- reaches out to women wherever they are;
- recognizes the need for women tutors;
- recognizes the needs of women tutors;
- rewards women tutors for their skills and commitment.

Women-friendly approaches to teaching and learning

In the second of the sources listed above, Gisela Pravda drew on the women-centred curriculum paper, among others, to provide a comprehensive attempt to analyse some of the components of women-only provision. In her analysis she uses the headings – the programme, the course content, the learning process, teacher behaviour, and the design and production of materials. Hers is essentially a theoretical analysis of women-only provision – an overview of selected sources – but it is based on a wide range of practice. What is particularly interesting is that her own work was with women in South America and that she included Spanish-speaking sources. From the analysis she has made it is apparent that the emerging characteristics of a 'women's curriculum' transcend national and language barriers as well as types of provision. Her analysis, which is included as Appendix 1, provides an alternative framework for the analysis of provision as well as guidelines for good practice.

This chapter has given an overview of the characteristics of women's education and the practicalities which must be addressed in good provision if the needs of women students are to be met. While some of the details in the guidelines are applicable only to women's education, many of the recommendations need to be recognized by any provider of education who wishes to welcome adult students, particularly women. Colleges of further education and institutions of higher education could well examine their provision using these lists as appropriate.

6 | The Curriculum of Women-only Provision – Six Case Studies

The two examples of curriculum analysis referred to in the last chapter have been theoretical, though drawn from practice. The methodology of 'grounded theory' was the approach adopted in a research project funded by the Further Education Unit (FEU) where six examples of different kinds of women-only provision were examined in detail and over a period of time. From these observations and other collected materials, my colleague Gill Goodchild and I drew up a framework for analysis which could be used both as an analytical tool and as a checklist or guide to good practice. This, and the following two chapters draw heavily on the unpublished report of the project (Coats et al. 1988).

Although the FEU had carried out some research into courses for women, there had been very little investigation into their curriculum. An early FEU study by Stoney and Reid (1980) looked at the role of 'bridging' courses for women and made recommendations about them. Later FEU publications, *Balancing the Equation* (Stoney and Reid 1981) and *Changing the Focus* (FEU 1984), raised issues relating to the provision and to the position of women in education but said little about the content and design of women-only courses.

The FEU project (Coats et al. 1988) originated from the East Midlands Women's Forum, a network group linked to the regional Replan staff development committee. The Forum had produced a document entitled *Consulting Women* (Coats 1988a) which collected a series of case studies of provision for women in the region, looking at the way groups were recruited, the negotiation of the curriculum, the problems encountered and the teaching methods used on the courses. The emphasis was on informal work carried out in the community. These case studies formed a useful base from which the FEU project developed. Although the earlier study essentially described the curriculum, it made no systematic attempt to analyse it. It took no recognition of the values which informed the design of the provision, of the constraints which affected its implementation, or of the need for assessment and evaluation.

The aims of the FEU project were:

- To analyse and appraise the curriculum design, course content and methods of teaching and learning on women-only courses.
- To identify the benefits and disadvantages of women-only provision.
- To supply guidelines for providers on the development of women-only courses.

Outline of the research

To enable an in-depth investigation of provision to be carried out, a research coordinator and two research workers selected six case studies of various types of provision, located in different areas of the country. The research was spread over a period of 18 months so that it was possible to follow through courses for a whole academic year or several shorter courses as appropriate.

The research was based at South Nottinghamshire College of Further Education and carried out between May 1988 and November 1989. The research team consisted of a research director (Peter Moseley, then principal of South Nottinghamshire College), a project coordinator (Joyce Deere) and two project officers (Maggie Coats and Gill Goodchild). The six case studies were chosen to provide a range of the main types of women-only provision in different geographical contexts and targeting different groups of women. One criterion for selection was that their funding was secure enough for the provision to continue throughout the research period. Another criterion was that they had a reputation for good practice, although this was a subjective judgement. Of the six case studies, three were courses based in FE colleges in very different locations – a large city, an industrial northern town and an area of mining decline. The courses concerned were a 'Women into Management' course, a NOW course and an access course. The three other studies were of a WEA branch's community based 'Return to Learn' provision, a women's technology centre and a long-term residential college for women. One of the strengths of this project was the collaboration between the researchers, the steering committee of the project, the tutors and the women in all the case studies selected.

Methodology

The research, which was carried out over a period of 18 months, used qualitative, interpretative and interactive methodology based on the following four tenets:

- The research could not be seen as a process towards the ultimate truth, although indicators of good practice may well emerge;
- The research model must allow feedback to take place. If the process was about exploring interpretations, then the model must be flexible enough to take account of those interpretations – it must therefore be a dynamic model;
- There must be a place for values within the model;
- The place of the women subjects of the research must be central.

Figure 6.1 Research model

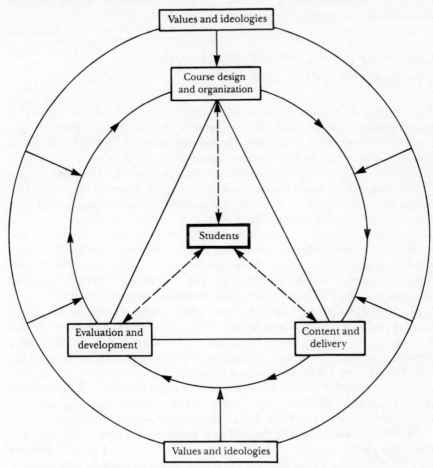

Source: Coats *et al.* (1988)

The resulting research model is shown in Figure 6.1. It is circular, allowing each stage to affect the whole cycle; the place of the students is central and the whole model is informed by values and ideology. The origin and the development of the three boxes of the research process were a result of integrating the findings from the project with other research models.

Description of the six case studies of women's education

The following details are taken from the full report (Coats *et al.* 1988) although the identity of the case studies has been removed. As the research was carried out in 1988–9, all the descriptions are presented in the past tense, which reflects the details at the time. In some cases these details have not changed and the provision continues as described.

Case study 1: A New Opportunities for Women (NOW) course

The original NOW course at this FE college was devised by a group of women tutors and the early courses involved several tutors, each making a particular contribution. Over time, the number involved had been reduced so that only two tutors took the main responsibility for design and delivery of the course, one of whom was part of the original group. In addition to women's studies and personal development components, taken by the two NOW tutors, all women took an 'Introduction to Computing' course, tutored by a woman from the computing department.

In addition to NOW and the follow-on NOW Two course, the college also provided women's studies modules, validated by a local open college federation – a women's studies course, a 'Women's Access to Information Technology' (WAIT) course, 'Women into Science and Technology' (WIST) courses, 'Women and the Law' and a women's workshop for practical skills.

The NOW courses were available three times a year, starting in September, January and April. Each course lasted one term of approximately 10–11 weeks, depending on the length of the term. The classes were held every Wednesday between 9.30 and 3.30, although women could leave at 3.00 if necessary. Half term breaks were taken to fit school terms.

The course had to have a minimum of 12 women enrolled and a maximum of 16. In practice most courses involved 14–15 women, although numbers were likely to vary each week due to women's changing circumstances.

The college had a crèche for children between two and a half and five years, but places were limited (16 for the whole college) and women applying for a NOW course could not be guaranteed a crèche place.

The course was free to women on benefit, dependent on a partner on benefit or holding a UB40. Fees in 1988 were approximately £2 per day – £20–22 per course. There was no crèche charge for women who did not pay course fees; other women paid 92p per session.

Aims and objectives

The aims and objectives of the NOW course were stated as:

1. To build a secure and cohesive group of local women where issues, concerns and ideas can be shared in an atmosphere of openness, trust and support;

2. To give the participants the opportunity to recognize their skills, practise them, build on them and, in certain areas, develop new skills;
3. To provide opportunities for members of the group to widen their expectations;
4. To foster an atmosphere where participation and cooperation are valued;
5. To provide a (re)introduction to learning and to develop the participants' learning skills;
6. To enhance self-esteem and to encourage each student to look to the future positively from within a supportive environment.

By the end of the course the participants will:

- be aware of what it is to be assertive and to use such skills when appropriate,
- be aware of their own skills and value,
- be able to communicate appropriately in various modes,
- take a positive and cooperative approach to other students,
- be open to ideas,
- have had the opportunity to meet women from a variety of backgrounds,
- be able to use a computer and have some knowledge of information technology,
- have spent some time in a one to one relationship with a tutor,
- have had the opportunity of a residential experience,
- have some plans for the future.

Publicity and recruitment

Publicity was by leaflets and posters using all the usual outlets, local papers (advertisements and articles), and local radio. There had been two 'open days' in college. A new outreach community tutor had been appointed by the college with responsibility for working with women. One major place of referral was the adjacent Educational Guidance Service for Adults (EGSA); women had also come from the Job Centre and other advisory agencies.

The demand for the course had been high with the possible exception of the summer term, when fewer people look for new educational provision. The tutors were currently looking for ways to publicize the course more widely, possibly using a video made by NOW students.

Enquiries could be by phone, letter or in person. All the women who enquired about the course were given details and an application form. The tutors tried to talk to enquirers if possible to check that NOW was appropriate for them. Although it was aimed mainly at women who had few or no qualifications, women with O levels or above were accepted if the provision seemed right for them. Priority was given to those women who were taking their first step back into education. Others were redirected to more appropriate courses.

Reception and registration

A small sign at the entrance gave the name of the college but the reception was not easy to find. The letter of acceptance sent to students before the course began gave full details of which building it was in and said they would be met on the first day in the foyer.

The room used by the NOW course was not easy to find. Most of the course took place in a room designated for women's studies but it had other uses. It was windowless, airless and hot – it had been a storeroom. Coffee and lunch were taken in the same room. The kettle and cups had to be removed each time but a small collection of books remained.

Registration was done during the first morning but not as the first task. Women were given a chance to settle down and begin to get to know the tutors and each other before filling in forms.

Students

The women on the NOW courses came from a large radius around the town but not usually from the nearby city. Some women had a considerable journey, involving walking and public transport. Others cycled or lived nearby; a few had the use of a car. Some came together sharing transport.

The women who attended NOW courses represented a wide age range – late teens to late 50s and even above. Most had children and almost all had been in a full-time domestic role for some time; a few had part-time jobs. Several were facing major changes in their circumstances – the end of a marriage or relationship, partner's redundancy or illness, children becoming less dependent on them. Some women were themselves recovering from periods of physical or mental illness or distressing family events.

Content of the course

The NOW course had three main components as well as other additional inputs. Each morning was divided into two sessions, separated by a coffee break. One tutor took the first session, entitled 'Women's Studies' which included, in the first part of the course, an examination of childhood, adolescence, work, marriage and family. This was followed by sessions on self-assessment, sifting options and making action plans for the future. After coffee each week the other tutor took the 'Personal Development' session. This consisted of a number of activities which were designed to enhance self-image and self-confidence; all used the support of the group to do this. Sessions started with a group-building or trust exercise; other issues covered included an examination of why it was a women-only course, assertiveness, putdowns, coping with criticism etc. Each course ended with an appraisal and a party.

Each lunch time women brought their own food which was eaten in the women's studies room. After eating, a range of lunch time speakers, from both inside and outside the college introduced topics of general interest or of direct relevance to the women. Those taking part included a numeracy tutor, a local magistrate, a local woman author etc.

In the afternoon there was an 'Introduction to Computing' class where women had hands-on experience and an introduction to word processing, spreadsheets and databases. The aim was not to master the operations as such but to give the women some understanding of what computing involves, to demystify the operation and to discover if they might wish to take the course further.

Finally, each day ended with a review session where women were encouraged to look back at the day and identify both good and bad points. This enabled the tutors to monitor the course and to identify areas of difficulty or changes which needed to be made.

In addition to the day's classes, each woman on the course was offered an individual tutorial with a tutor so that her future plans could be identified. More information or contacts could be organized for women who needed further advice.

The other important component of the course was the residential weekend at a nearby adult college. This was open to all the women and as many as possible attended. Child care was available for those unable to leave their children; there was no cost for the weekend.

The programme for the weekend was devised by the NOW tutors and students, together with the staff of the college. Most women felt some trepidation at going away from home and it was important that they knew what to expect. Even then the experience was a significant one for most of them; many had not been away without their families for many years, if at all.

Methodology

All the course sessions were based on group activities with the exception of computing. Even here the support of the group was evident, although the computing tasks had to be individually performed. Most sessions began with the sharing of experiences in a series of group exercises which worked towards a group identity and cohesion. Most activities were carried out in pairs or subgroups, with the whole group sharing or reporting back. Flip charts were prepared, displayed and presented. Discussions of issues encouraged participation but without pressure; women were not exposed against their will, especially those with learning problems. Handouts were used but often displayed on the over-head projector, read and discussed beforehand so that the tasks were clear.

Guidelines for group discussion were drawn up with the group and these were gently but firmly enforced. Sharing experiences and opinions was encouraged; each woman's contribution was valued. The emphasis was on description and not explanation. There was little reference to theory although the rationale for activities was explained.

Progression

The wide range of courses offered by the college, together with open learning facilities, meant that most women could find something they wished to do when the NOW course ended. In addition, for those on the autumn or spring NOW courses, there was the possibility of continuing on a NOW Two course, if sufficient numbers were interested. These courses were based on project work around issues chosen by the women and presented in any form they chose. It provided small groups of women with the chance to follow up a topic in more depth, as well as having the opportunity to experiment with audio-visual media if they wished.

However, some groups did not find it easy to agree on a topic or devise more independent ways of working. Although both tutors were available for guidance and advice, the very supportive role they played in NOW One was lessened. In theory this was good, as women had to develop the ability to move on with greater independence but not all were able to cope with it. An alternative provision which was very successful was that, for one group, NOW Two focused more on specific skills in preparation for further study, training or work. This included more work on basic study skills, as well as c.v. preparation and interviewing techniques.

Assessment and evaluation

Since the course included no formal assessment of students or evaluation of the provision, it would have been easy to stagnate and become repetitive. That this was not so was mainly due to the sensitivity of the tutors to the needs of the students, reinforced by a strong commitment to the standard of the course they provided. Constant informal discussion, both during and between courses, meant that modifications could and were made. Each group of NOW women developed in a different way and responding to this was important; what worked wonderfully with one group might prove entirely inappropriate with another. Despite the demands of their timetables and the distance between their departments, the fact that the two tutors were both colleagues and friends meant that their work was constantly reviewed.

It would have been possible for this course to be validated under an open college federation scheme but both tutors rejected this possibility. Indeed, any external accountability would have placed some restraint on their flexibility. A head of department who clearly respected their autonomy reinforced the obvious quality of this provision.

What particular lessons can be learned from this case study?

1. These NOW courses had clear aims and objectives (see above). The courses were designed to meet these and they achieved them.

2. Despite the considerable differences in the age, background and circumstances of the women on any one course, the tutors managed to create a supportive and caring group which persisted even after the course had finished.

3. The relationship between points 1 and 2 above – and the success of the course generally – could be attributed to the considerable group skills of the two main tutors and their ability to relate to the women concerned.

4. The residential weekend was a major experience for the women who attended, despite the fact that most of them had not been away from home before. Again, the skills of the tutors and those of the staff of the adult college were responsible for the success of this.

5. The tutors' sensitivity to the needs of the particular group meant that subtle changes could be made to the programme and to activities/exercises within any session. No two NOW courses were exactly the same.

6. The course struck a balance between the sharing of personal experiences, which can be emotive and intense, and the need for controlled support. Women were not put under pressure to contribute.

7. The content of the course explored the students' identities and roles both as persons and as women but did not uncomfortably challenge either. For example, the ethos was not anti-men or anti-marriage.

8. Progression was seen as a major issue and there were lots of options within the college. The tutors were aware that some women did 'slip away' during or at the end of a course but information and advice was always available, both in college and through the local EGSA.

Case study 2: WEA 'Return to Learn' and 'Getting on with Maths' courses

These courses were held on several large council estates, which lay on the outskirts of a historic city. Many of the estates were isolated and lacking in facilities; communications were poor, making access to the centre of the city very difficult. Although the average unemployment figure for the city in 1988 was around 3 per cent, on these estates it was much higher. There were very few educational opportunities for women on these estates, although the city as a whole was well provided.

History of provision for women

This branch of the WEA was committed to making educational provision available for working-class women, free of charge and with a free crèche. Their original courses were called 'A Time for Yourself' and were located on different estates. The courses were informal and flexible, giving women a chance to meet and discuss a whole range of topics. However, this flexibility also led to fragmentation and some provision became nothing more than a series of single sessions, often with an outside speaker. As groups began to stagnate it became more difficult to find new topics; it also became more difficult to find new members. There was no sense of progression or growth.

Despite an attempt to use coherent 'themes' for each course, it became apparent that the resources were not reaching more women nor being used effectively. Thus the provision was restructured, renamed and moved into other locations although the original aims remained unchanged.

'Return to Learn' (RTL) and 'Getting on with Maths' courses

In 1988 the new model for the courses was called 'Return to Learn' and in 1989 a different version, 'Getting on with Maths' was tried. During the research period four courses were visited – three RTL and one maths – held in local community centres on different estates. All courses lasted for 13–14 weeks, one day a week between 9.30 and 11.30. Crèche facilities for babies and preschool children were provided in a room nearby; both the course and the child care were free. If insufficient crèche places were available, a child care allowance was paid to those who wished to make their own arrangements. The courses started at different times in the year and took breaks for school half-terms and holidays. The WEA branch received funding from the city council and the county council.

Aims and objectives

All the courses were aimed at women who had few or no formal qualifications. The leaflet advertising the RTL courses said that it aimed to:

- brush up your learning skills – note taking, writing, reading and discussion;
- develop your confidence;
- look at topics of interest to you, such as education, health, race, family, welfare rights;
- help you decide what you would like to go on to next.

Publicity and recruitment

Publicity was by leaflets which were widely distributed on the relevant estate and through local schools. Whenever possible, outreach activities were carried out by local women.

The leaflets told women what to expect and what the course would consist of:

a pre-course meeting to meet each other, your two tutors and the crèche workers, with your children (if you are bringing them to the crèche);

thirteen weeks, two hours a week with free child care; two one-to-one sessions with your tutor (to be arranged); a small amount of work for you to do between classes – about two hours a week.

The leaflet contained a reply slip indicating interest and telephone numbers for further information. Women who returned the slip were invited to the pre-course meeting and, after discussing their suitability, completed a simple application form. Women for whom the course seemed unsuitable – women with good qualifications for example – were redirected elsewhere.

Students

For the four courses followed during the research period, there was a total of 45 student application forms. The three RTL courses attracted women of all ages, mainly from the locality concerned. The maths course – the only one of its kind held during the year – drew women from a wider area. All three RTL courses had black women in them – Afro-Caribbean women and women from overseas whose husbands were studying or working in the city.

The information gathered from the 45 forms could be summarized thus:

- Ages: Ages ranged from 20 to 56, with most of the women in their 20s or 30s; about half (22 out of 45) were between 30 and 40.
- Education: Sixteen women gave no details of exams or qualifications; four more stated that they had none at all. Of the rest, 14 out of 45 had no GCE O levels but had something else, mostly CSEs or RSAs. Eleven women said they had one or more O level passes but only one woman listed more than five. This confirmed that the courses were attracting the women for whom they were designed.
- Work done: As with other case studies in this research, this question elicited a list of all the traditional women's low-paid jobs – clerical work, retail and catering, cleaning or care, and factory work. Very few mentioned a job involving training – a couple of nurses, a VDU operator etc.
- Current work: Whilst there was some confusion over the label 'unemployed' and 'unwaged', it was apparent that only a few of the women were currently in paid work outside of the home; seven women listed part-time jobs.
- Reasons for coming on the course: For all the RTL courses the most common reason related to confidence, although this was not mentioned by the maths students. Other reasons were equally shared – to get skills towards a future job, to compensate for schooling, for personal gain. Of the specific skills mentioned, improved English was common, especially spelling.

Some of the courses gave students a further form where they could indicate the kind of things they wanted to cover in the course. Responses to the first question 'What I want from this course is . . .' provided additional information about the expressed needs of the women but the same concerns emerged:

- 'To gain more confidence and be able to talk to people';
- 'Confidence and a chance to further my education and gain new skills';
- 'Just a little help to start me thinking about me as a person and what I can do';
- 'I want to get my confidence and find something to do with my future';
- 'Education, being more assertive, speaking out more';
- 'Maths; confidence; English'.

For the women on the maths course, the reasons given were much more instrumental:

- 'Brush up my maths with a view to taking GCSE';
- 'Always wanted to improve my maths; always thought I could do better';
- 'Improve my standard of education';
- 'I want to improve my grasp of maths to help my children and also attempt to pass my O level';
- 'To prepare for an access course that's due to start in September';
- 'To get up to date with maths'.

Content of the courses

All the RTL courses operated with a common framework and intention but differed in their content and delivery. Components in common included a commitment to shared learning but operated by negotiation with the students; coverage of certain study skills but delivered through different subject matter. Each course began by discussing what should be covered, both skills and topics, and by devising guidelines for group behaviour. Skills could include reading and writing, note taking, clear thinking, discussion and debate, analysis of television, some simple numeracy and the use of a library. On the earlier courses individual projects had been attempted but this was then replaced by a class magazine.

Not all the courses had one unifying theme; some seemed to have several themes or to operate with diverse topics. Work was done on women and health, current affairs, TV soap operas, advertising, religious education and other issues.

The maths course, not surprisingly, had a much narrower focus and covered a series of mathematical topics, depending on the level of individuals in the group. Long division seemed to be a common problem (calculators were used), plus work on fractions, decimals, percentages etc. Most, but not all of the material came from the ALBSU Numeracy Pack, which was purchased by most of the women, at their request.

Methodology

Each meeting of the RTL courses began with a group sharing exercise, not too personal or threatening but providing an opportunity for everyone to contribute. Work then focused on a different skill, embedded in appropriate content. Sometimes the women worked on a task in pairs or subgroups; at other times the whole group engaged in the same task. Stimulus materials were used – books, work sheets, visual materials, even Smarties chocolate sweets. There was a balance between encouraging participation and not being coercive, since clearly some women were more articulate and confident than others.

All sessions were cotutored, with each tutor taking responsibility for part of the time. Although clearly each partnership was different and pairs of tutors exhibited different strengths and preferred methods of working, there was no overt tension.

The maths tutor had devised a pattern for each session that included some shared working – in pairs or the whole group – followed by individual work and finally, a shared exercise to finish. The relatively light-hearted puzzles and quizzes done together not only made maths appear fun but also diffused any potential competitiveness and encouraged cooperation. Thus the middle section, where women worked individually at their own pace, was not threatening and weaknesses were not exposed. It was also noticeable that the women helped each other and some worked in pairs, thus making the task of the tutor, who tried to get round to each woman in turn, a little less demanding. Some work was done as a demonstration on the 'board' (a rather inconvenient flip chart without a proper black or white board) but for a group of up to 16 women this was necessary.

Progression

Progress was difficult to gauge since there was no formal way of following up students who completed any of the courses.

RTL courses were devised as a first step back into study for those women who thought they were ready to return and had some sort of intention to continue. The focus was primarily on return to learn and the expectation was that progression would be to more education. However, women who opted not to continue or to look for training or employment were not seen as 'failures' and their right to determine their own future was respected.

The course included a very detailed session on future options which covered all the opportunities for further study available in the area. Overall there was probably more on offer than anywhere else outside London, although cost, child care and lack of mobility may have restricted the choice for many women.

Although the actual amount of skill work that could be covered in a brief course such as this had to be fairly superficial, nevertheless two requirements for successful progression were included. The first was increased confidence. Given the number of women who stated that as their prime need, the shared learning which enhanced confidence and the rediscovery of skills encouraged many to continue. The first step back is always the most difficult and for working-class women with very limited qualifications this was supportive and appropriate provision. The second requirement was simply knowing where to go for more information on what was available and having some kind of guidance and advice to help decide. Again the courses provided this guidance.

The maths course was different, although clearly many women did intend to continue as their stated reasons for coming have shown.What did need to be explored was the importance of this experience for confidence enhancement. Even quite small progress in terms of mathematical understanding, accompanied by the demystifying of the subject and making it accessible, had immense benefits, although these would be hard to assess. The environment replaced memories of competition and failure. The importance of all this help and support of a maths 'teacher' who was sensitive and encouraging helped women to overcome earlier unpleasant experiences. The cooperative and non-threatening environment can replace memories of competition and failure. The importance of this for progression has to be recognized.

Assessment and evaluation

Since all of this provision carried no formal assessment of students or external validation, other criteria for monitoring and feedback had to be devised. Individual students were encouraged to see their potential strengths and to make a realistic appraisal of themselves before moving on; the individual tutorials were designed to be part of this process. Feedback by the students was more difficult to ascertain although an opportunity was provided for this.

Evaluation by the tutors was encouraged both as an ongoing process and in their final report. Less formal but equally effective were the discussions at the tutors' meetings where more general issues were raised.

One example of this was the question of including individual project work. Some concern had been expressed that introducing projects had led some women to withdraw from courses; that project work took up a great deal of time; that the choice of topics by women was not always wise; and that quite a number of projects were never completed. On the other hand, the value of individual project work as a learning experience could be very important and the sense of enjoyment and achievement felt by those who did complete work had been recognized. The discussion amongst tutors allowed for these and other issues to be debated. A decision to try compiling a class magazine to which all women could contribute was made.

Finally, it must be recognized that this provision had to be evaluated each year for the benefit of the funding body. Since grants were made under 'access' criteria, it was essential that both the progression of students and assessment and monitoring of the provision were taken seriously.

What particular lessons can be learned from this case study?

1. This provision was quite clear in determining its target group as working-class women with few or no formal qualifications and it was apparent that it was reaching those women. It was also apparent that women in this category were serious about returning to education and were eager to

learn. Above all they valued the skills needed and were keen to develop them.

2. At the same time many of the women recognized their lack of confidence and wanted to (re)gain this. It was not easy to devise a programme which focused on the need to develop individual skills at the same time as providing a supportive and non-threatening learning environment, and yet it was the combination of the two – skills and support – that led to enhanced confidence.

3. This provision also illustrated another tension – the ability to allow negotiation within a framework. On the one hand it was important to avoid the structureless negotiation which allows some members of the group to dictate their wishes or the disparity that tries to satisfy the irreconcilable needs of everyone. On the other hand, a rigid structure which patterns a provision can ignore the needs of the students.

4. There can be no doubt about the enormous benefit of cotutoring this kind of course, even though the difficulties also had to be acknowledged. Pairs of tutors who could work through potential conflict to produce a complementary team were able to support each other and the students in a much better way than even one very gifted tutor working alone.

5. The skills needed by tutors of this kind of provision had to be recognized. Not only did they need to be fully committed to the aims of the course but they needed certain personal characteristics if they were to help women from particularly disadvantaged backgrounds at the point of re-entry.

6. The recognition of this and of the demands of cotutoring were fully recognized in the terms and conditions offered to these part-time tutors. Payment for training meetings, for preparation and consultation and for individual tutorial provision signified the value placed by the WEA branch on these things. This had obvious implications for funding and resources but reflected too the priority of making good provision for both tutors and students.

Case study 3: Provision at an adult residential college for women

Of the eight adult long-term residential colleges in Britain, only one is for women only. The college is housed in a large Victorian mansion, with a newer residential block in its grounds, in the southeast of England. It attracts women from all over the country, although it is not surprising that the majority of the students – all the day students and some of the residents – come from the southeast.

History of the provision

The college was founded in 1920 to provide an educational opportunity for women who had not had such an opportunity earlier in life. It was designed to provide for any woman who demonstrated her ability to benefit from the provision. Like most of the long-term adult colleges, for some students it provided a route into higher education, although that was never its sole aim.

In the past few years there had been a change of emphasis both in the women it recruited and in the courses it offered. Although not departing from its traditional aim, it now sought to provide mainly for educationally disadvantaged women, in particular for working-class and black women. The provision had changed from a standard two year certificate to a modular course of one or two years, offering more choice and flexibility. In addition, shorter courses for women, both day and residential, had been developed.

The college was funded with a grant direct from the DES. Full-time students on the CNAA certificate courses had their fees paid and were entitled to a mandatory grant.

Courses at this college

The main provision was the one or two year modular course leading to a CNAA Certificate in Higher Education in Combined Studies or Social Studies. Each year was divided into two semesters (September to February; February to June) during which students had to choose three assessed and one complementary (unassessed) module. The CNAA certificates could be awarded after one year or two years of study.

The research focused on these long courses for full-time residential, full-time day and associate (part-time day) students. In addition to this provision, the college had developed a series of short courses of various types. A number of the students on the short courses went on to become full-time students there.

In all, the certificate courses catered for 70 students at any one time, both first and second years; the number who stayed for a second year had decreased over the last few years. About 50 women were resident, the remainder were full-time day students who lived locally and for whom residence would be impossible. Associate students could 'purchase' up to two assessed and two complementary modules at any time, providing that there was space in the relevant class. Associate students could accumulate these modules towards a certificate.

Aims and objectives

A submission by the college to the CNAA stated:

It is primarily concerned to recruit women who have missed educational opportunities earlier in life and who now wish to clarify their own educational and vocational requirements through study and consider their options for the future. From the start of the course, the College emphasises the importance of helping students in the diagnosis of future needs.

In addition, the importance of residence was stressed. It was argued that a full-time residential course was a necessary requirement because it allowed for increased labour mobility, increased personal and social skills, increased powers of reflection, self-analysis and self-knowledge and for interaction with day students. Students who were resident spoke of the enormous advantage of being free from domestic responsibilities and able to concentrate unhindered on their study.

A list of objectives for the college stated that, at the end of the period of study:

Students will have acquired:

- a broad intellectual background
- self expression, oral and written skills
- organizational and analytical skills
- numeracy skills
- appreciation of new technology
- word processing skills
- information retrieval skills
- self presentation skills
- self assessment skills and the capacity to direct their own future.

Publicity and recruitment

As a national institution, the college faced the difficult task of making its provision known to those women for whom it might be suitable. While it was listed in all the main books and directories which cover educational opportunities for adults, it is fair to say that the college and what it had to offer was not generally known amongst women themselves. The students were emphatic about the need to advertise more widely. Educational and vocational agencies knew of its existence but not all women had access to them. Advertisements in national papers were used but it was not surprising to find that most women learned about the college from friends or contacts or from other educational providers.

All enquirers and applicants were invited to attend an informal interview if they wished, followed by a formal one if they decided to make a firm application. There were no stated requirements except that women must be 21 years of age or above; there was no upper age limit.

The selection criteria as stated by the college were that:

Students should:

- have a high degree of motivation towards study over a one or two year period;
- demonstrate the need for the course, i.e. show a desire to reappraise their capabilities and change direction and an ability for self-appraisal; indicate they could benefit from a residential course academically and personally;

- have few or no formal qualifications;
- have no suitable alternative course of study, for example an access course;
- provide references relating to previous part-time study, employment or voluntary activities;
- take part in an interview at the College;
- undertake a written test at the time of interview;
- in the case of students wishing to prepare for social work, have some experience or evidence of aptitude in the broad field of social welfare.

Those students who wished to apply for the Certificate in Social Studies option were designated as 'social work students' which signified their intention to enter social work or a related caring profession. They were interviewed with this in mind and were expected to have some relevant experience.

As a result of the interview procedure, women were either offered a place at the college or offered a place subject to certain requirements being met, e.g. deferred for a year to take a preparatory course. Women for whom the college was not considered appropriate were given information and advice about other provision.

Reception and registration

The nature of the college and the complexity of course choice meant that time had to be allocated to this process at the beginning of each college year. All women on the full-time course attended 'induction days' in September. In addition to becoming familiar with college routine, the main activity centred on allocation to tutor groups and choice of modules for the first semester.

The great advantage of a modular system was that it gave students some control over the content of their study in that they could select from a wide range of subjects. Thus they were able to compile a profile which allowed for their interests as well as their future intentions. The disadvantage was that the wide range of options available made the choice difficult, particularly for the first semester when students did not know what each subject entailed or what their future plans might be. Advice was available to help students in their choices and to make sure their profile was coherent.

Students who were hoping to gain the Certificate in Combined Studies had greater flexibility than those who were aiming for the Social Studies option. Students who were accepted for this option were advised on their choices, which had to include certain social policy, sociology and psychology modules.

Students

Women came to the college from all over Britain and beyond, although all the day students, part-time students and some of the residents were from the surrounding area. They came for a whole range of reasons, but overwhelmingly with a desire to learn.

Women came from a wide range of backgrounds and different circumstances. Apart from the fact that all shared the disadvantage of having had poor educational experiences, many had faced other forms of discrimination and difficulty. Some were facing poverty and distress due to circumstances beyond their control; some had recent disruptions and unhappy events to cope with. Most were facing change in themselves and in their circumstances. All had to adjust to the new demands of serious study and the initially stressful demands of college life. The staff were aware of this and were sensitive to the pressures on their students.

Despite periods of panic and depression, most of the students demonstrated great motivation and a determination to succeed. The principal spoke of the tenacity, commitment and enthusiasm which led students both to apply in the first place and then to go on and succeed, reinforcing what she saw as the capability and infinite resources, both personal and intellectual, of many women. This college tried as much as any institution to foster this attitude and, as the results show, in most cases they were successful.

Content

It was difficult to summarize the content of the many modules available but some idea of the range of subjects could be gained from the module choice list:

Assessed Modules Semester One
Algebra; Art and Ideas; Drama in Society; Economic and Social Problems; Introduction to Sociology; Literature, Language and Imagination; Political Ideologies; Social Change 1851–1951; Social History 1700–1850; Sociology, Society and Social Issues; Women Welfare and Law; Word and Image I.

Assessed Modules Semester Two
Art in England; Computer Studies; Developmental Psychology; Deviance, Delinquency and Social Policy; Economic Policy; European History 1870–1914; Geometry; Statistical Methods of Social Investigation; Social Policy; Twentieth Century Drama; Varieties of the Novel; War and Society (Europe 1914); Word and Image II.

In addition, students could opt for a module in Independent Study or could 'module borrow' from another institution. Social work students also had an assessed placement. Complementary modules (unassessed but compulsory) included: Gallery Going; Making Sense of the Education System; Voluntary Social Work; Approaches to the Study of History; Introduction to Computers; Living with Science and Technology; Literature Workshops; Humanistic Psychology; Experiencing Architecture; Values in Society; Women, Work and Family; Imperialism; Philosophy; Social Psychology and Social Concerns; Mathematics.

Having made a choice of three assessed and one complementary module for each semester, students also took a range of core studies. These consisted of a programme of study skills, numeracy, career and educational planning and assertiveness training. Further study skill options were available to meet individual needs, as well as specific skills for different subject areas. Tutor groups met with their personal tutor on a regular basis.

In most of the modules and parts of the core studies, the content was prescribed. In the independent study option, however, individuals pursued an in-depth study of their own choice, assisted by an appropriate tutor and helped by resources provided by the college librarian.

Methodology

It was difficult to give a brief summary of the methods used to deliver the curriculum since there was considerable variety depending on both tutor and subject. The overall emphasis of the college was stated to be on student-centred learning, enabling women to take responsibility for their own learning and become independent and autonomous. Parts of the curriculum encouraged this, especially the core subjects. Some modules engaged students in reflective learning, drawing on their own experiences and locating that experience in a wider social context. However, in other modules the presentation was more traditional with an emphasis on academic content.

Again, some modules focused on the acquisition of skills and processes rather than the content of 'knowledge'. Traditional methods of presentation – lectures and note taking, essays and exams – sat alongside more participative and inventive approaches.

Progression

Progression was taken very seriously at the college. As explained above, one of the main aims was to enable women to make a realistic appraisal of their potential and to decide on a new direction or purpose. For most of the women that involved further education or training, mainly entry to degree or CQSW courses.

Until changed in 1989, it was customary for women who intended to move on to higher education to stay two years at the college before gaining the CNAA certificate. However, it became increasingly apparent that many women needed only one year of full-time study to reach the standard and readiness to progress. A successful submission was made to the CNAA to have the certificate requirement reduced to one year, with the option of a two year course for those who needed longer. That many women were accepted by HE institutions after one year, and in some cases, given entry to the second year of degree courses, demonstrated the adequacy of the two semester course rather than needing provision for four semesters. Given also the increasing number of other access courses which last one year, plus the high standards and the bonus of residence for these students, it seems more than reasonable that one year should be sufficient for most, but not for all; there were women who needed more time both for personal and for intellectual reasons. There is evidence to show that women from this college who progress to HE do extremely well, with low drop-out rate and considerable academic success. Given the retention issue for mature students in HE, the college compares very favourably with other access provision. It warns students that provision in HE may not recognize their particular requirements nor give the support they need; it empowers them to challenge traditional attitudes and equips them with the skills they will require.

This raised a major problem that is shared with many other institutions which provide 'access' routes into HE. The UCCA and PCAS process starts just as most students were trying to settle into the first phase of study and were not ready to make major decisions about their futures. Not only were many unsettled and unsure at this stage, but they also had insufficient experience either to have assessed their potential or to have discovered which subject areas most interested them. Until either the annual pattern is changed or the entry process modified for mature students, there seems to be no easy solution to this, other than to hope for late or changed applications to be accepted. This was one of the reasons why students at the college tended to think at the start of the course that they would need two years, only to discover by the following summer that they knew what they wanted to do and were ready then to proceed.

There were also women who eventually decided that further education was not appropriate for them and it was important to recognize their needs. To this end, the college encouraged women to make a realistic self-appraisal.

Assessment and evaluation

The assessment of students was carried out by both continuous assessment and by the end of module examinations, with an overall pass mark of 40 per cent. The balance between continuous assessment and exams varied according to the module but was usually 50/50. Complementary modules and core studies were 'assessed' by attendance only. Provision was made for students who failed individual module exams to retake them before moving on to other modules.

Assessment was carried out by the tutors concerned with each module, each of which had an external adviser. Under CNAA regulations, two other external examiners were appointed to moderate the certificate provision.

All the modules provided in both the first and second semesters, whether taken by first or second year students, were intended to be of equal standard. This presented a problem with continuous assessment for students in the first few weeks of their first modules. Although there was intensive help available with study skills, both in the core and within modules, many women felt that they were expected to submit graded work before they had the competence or confidence to do so. There was a sense of panic and distress when the first essays were due.

The module programme was the responsibility of the course coordinator, a post which rotated every two to three years. Policy matters were discussed at Academic Board, which was attended by all the staff and four elected student representatives.

There was a clearly defined cycle for evaluation and review at the college which involved both staff and students. At the end of each semester both staff and students reviewed the content and methods of each module. One to one staff/student feedback sessions were held to review progress and discuss future plans. At this point an examiners' meeting reported on both student progress and course developments. At the end of the second semester, as this was also the end of the academic year, an annual staff review was also held and an annual report compiled each July. Changes were discussed and the induction programme planned, in readiness for the new academic year.

What particular lessons can be learned from this case study?

1. It was possible for a considerable number of women from very educationally disadvantaged backgrounds to reach a good standard for entry, and subsequent successful completion of, degree courses in a wide range of universities, polytechnics and colleges of higher education.
2. It was possible to provide an academic curriculum in both content and method as long as the individual support and guidance needed by each woman was also provided.
3. It was possible for staff with a range of views to work together, providing opportunities for discussion and debate existed and clear aims and objectives for the provision were accepted.
4. The importance of the core programme could not be overemphasized.
5. There was enormous value in residential provision available for those women who were able to take advantage of it.
6. During times of stress and change, the provision of professional counselling, to supplement that offered by other staff, proved invaluable.
7. External validation of a course need not be a constraint and can ensure a rigorous check on standards. Submissions to the validating body demanded that issues were debated and agreed.
8. This institution is more than just a college providing access to HE; it is a unique centre for women's education and a valuable resource.

Case study 4: An access course for women

This access course seems to have resulted from a combination of two initiatives, one from a group of women and another later initiative from college management. A group of women who had been active in 'Women against Pit Closures' in 1984 came to the college in 1986 and expressed an interest in taking some courses. One of the responses to their request was that the woman responsible for curriculum development at the college was given the responsibility of planning a new women's access course. Once the developmental work was under way a course coordinator with a commitment to women's studies was appointed.

The course

This was a full-time, 36 week course. The hours were between 9.45 a.m. and 3.15 p.m., with the same holidays as the local schools. The course needed a minimum of 12 students and the retention rate was good. The college had a crèche for children over age two and a half and a nursery for younger children was being built. Priority in the crèche was given to women on the access course. In most cases there were no fees; full-time students received a minor award from the local education authority to cover fees, travel and expenses.

Aims and objectives

The course's aims and objectives can be seen in an extract from the course book:

> The course is intended to meet the needs of women in the villages which compose the mining community surrounding the college. The general features of women's educational background which are in evidence in society as a whole are noticeably prevalent in this particular industrial and geographical setting . . . The needs of such a variety of students indicate that it is necessary to provide a course for women from the age of 19 upwards, which will be sufficiently flexible to allow for a number of different exits, such as FE, HE or work . . . It is intended that the curriculum design will give access to a broad range of degree courses in the humanities and social sciences. The emphasis of the course is on the development of the intellectual skills of evaluation and criticism . . . The needs of adults returning to education to be able to base their studies on topics relevant to them has been of primary concern . . . Since women students returning to education have usually done so out of a need to make some 'fresh start' a community placement has been arranged . . . The development of study skills is taken very seriously.

Publicity and recruitment

Publicity was by leaflets and posters, but the most effective recruitment was through the various community and educational groups which met in the area and were part of the outreach work of the college. Some women heard about the course whilst on a 'second chance' course which ran during the summer term.

Prospective students were invited to get in touch with the course coordinator and her friendly response was welcomed. She wrote a personal letter in reply to each enquiry and met and talked to every woman before starting the course.

Reception and registration

There were a number of entrances to the college and none seemed more 'main' than others. Reception was signposted but not easy to find, being in the middle of the site. The access course had its own base room in an annexe to the main college, which was once part of an old school. The room was well heated, had a sink, kettle, pin board, blackboard, storage cupboards, a coat rail, a typewriter for student use and an adjacent lavatory. The base room was mentioned by students as one of the reasons they had found it easy to re-enter education. The women had coffee and lunch in the room, brought their children there in the lunch hour and left their belongings there if they had to go elsewhere in the college. Classes not requiring specialist equipment were carried out in this room. Other classes were in the art room, the computer room or open learning centre.

Students

The women on the course were a group who saw the course as a way out. The reasons they gave for joining the course emphasized the importance of education and most were hoping to go on to more study when the course was over. The course seemed to have been seen as compensating for what they had missed earlier in their education. Most of the women were white and from a working class background.

Content of the course

The course was divided into six main areas, each with two complementary groupings:

Human studies: People in society, women's studies;
Science and technology: Science in our lives, computers in society;
Historical/critical studies: Economic and social history, creative studies;
Basic skills: English, maths;
Support: Personal and social education, individual and group tutorials.

The days were generally divided into two sessions, before and after lunch, except for Wednesday which was placement day. A group tutorial for half an hour started each week on Monday mornings and individual tutorials took place on Tuesday mornings, just before lunch.

There was also a residential weekend at an adult college. Some tutors went along to this session. Some children went too, which was seen as an advantage (in that women did not have to find alternative care) and a disadvantage (in that it would have been nice to get away alone). The programme for the weekend was chosen by the students themselves and the whole experience was important in solidifying the group feeling.

Methodology

Whenever possible the starting point was life experience and the intention was to generate self-confidence and motivation. Consequently the course was process orientated and focused on the development of both study skills and analytical ability. The emphasis was on student-centred learning, providing the student with opportunities to develop her potential. Cooperation was encouraged between students in order to move them away from the idea of individualized learning.

The maths and English work took place in the open learning workshop, with students working at their own pace but helping one another. In other subject areas a typical session consisted of the tutor giving out a piece of work which served as a focus for discussion. The women were then expected to do a lot of follow-up work in their own time. In many of the sessions there was an explicit attempt to bring the discussion around to an analysis in terms of the women's position in society and to move the discussion from a descriptive to an analytical level. The computer class was an exception to this method in that it was more individually focused but the women were supportive of each other in discussing computing in more informal talks.

Progression

From the first two years of the course several women had moved on to HE, several had gone on to other courses at the college and some had gone on to do GCSE Maths, with the intention of going on to BEd courses. Most seemed to consider the issue of moving on to mixed provision to be a minor irritation with which they felt prepared to cope, having gained confidence on the women-only course. One remaining tension was that between being a wife and mother while embarking on these courses. For some that had been a difficulty all year and they felt it would not be easy to sort this problem out. All the women felt they had moved forward from where they had started the course.

Assessment and evaluation

This aspect was one of the many strengths of the access course. The course was externally validated by a local open college federation and the outcome was a recognized access route to HE. In the two years it had been offered, students had gained access to four different institutions. The course was taught, assessed and accredited according to three different levels of the open college validation scheme. The assessment was carried out by student/tutor negotiation of 'positive statement banks' – a system of competence statements against which students and staff could assess student progress.

In addition to the assessment and validation of students, the course was evaluated by both students and staff. There were course team meetings, which student representatives attended, held at monthly intervals; this formed one dimension of course evaluation. The other two were by discussion in group tutorials throughout the year and by questionnaire. The information from these three sources was considered seriously in subsequent course development and resulted in modifications in content being made.

What particular lessons can be learned from this case study?

1. The access course tutor was very emphatic about the need to interview all the students in depth before the course began. This was to establish the student's suitability for the courses, the course's suitability for her, and to look at any potential practical problems (e.g. child care, travel, finance).
2. The course's handbook was an excellent document – all-embracing, professionally presented and of great help to the students.
3. The base room was seen by students and staff alike as an important resource – especially as somewhere to take children at lunch time.
4. Similarly, the travel arrangements were seen as an important facility. Coming from scattered communities, the provision of a taxi for some students was crucial in enabling them to attend.
5. The course was a response to an expressed need of local women. It grew out of what they wanted and their views were taken into account as the course developed.
6. The response to the first enquiry from a woman was seen as very important. The women were heartened by the response they received; it made the course seem a friendly place to be.
7. The community placement gave women the experience of going out into the world of paid work. Sometimes they went in pairs initially, until their confidence developed.
8. The residential weekend was an asset, both in reinforcing group solidarity and in building confidence.
9. The fact that the course was validated by a local open college federation was accepted as a real qualification by HE institutions and was important in boosting confidence. It meant that completing this access course was seen as respectable.
10. The commitment, kindness and tenacity of the tutor in charge of the course, sometimes at odds with those in authority, was critical.

Case study 5: A Women into Management course at an FE college

This college had, for a number of years, offered a variety of courses for women. When ESF money became available for a Women into Management course, the city council asked the college to provide it.

The course

The course was full-time (30 hours per week), between 9.30 and 4.30 and ran for 14 weeks between October and February. There was a half term and two weeks holiday at Christmas to coincide with school holidays. The course needed a minimum of 12 students and at the time of the research had 15. The college had a crèche for children between two and a half and five years but by the time recruitment for the management course took place it was full. Childminder and nursery fees were paid and there was a school pick-up allowance of £2 per hour for up to two hours a day. There were no course fees and a training allowance of £38 per week was paid if a woman was on benefit, plus weekly travel.

Aims and objectives

Aims were stated as:

* to develop management skills;
* to enable trainees to use computer skills relevant to management;
* to enable the trainees to identify a suitable career plan, to find employment or to enter FE;
* to build confidence;
* to update or build on existing skills.

The overall aim was to

> enable women who have previously held managerial or supervisory posts, or who are capable of doing so, to return to work in similar level jobs, or identify suitable training which will enable them to do so.

Publicity and recruitment

The course was publicized in local papers, outreach centres, libraries and in community groups. Local radio was also used, including the local Afro-Caribbean radio station. Most students found out about the course either from the newspaper or from contacting the college. There were some problems with recruitment in that there was little time between the course being given to the college, the developmental work being completed and the start of the course. All the women had a short interview with the course tutor to ascertain the suitability of the course for them and their suitability for the course. This may be one of the points where difficulties began to emerge, with a possible mismatch between the expectations of the students and what the course was designed to provide. Several of the women had O levels before starting the course; others had A levels; two had degrees and two had supervisory qualifications. One woman left work to come on the course.

Reception and registration

The college itself was easy to find, but the reception area less so. The reception area itself was rather bleak – an empty area with a television monitor providing up to the minute information and a security guard were the two main impressions received. There was in fact a receptionist but on several visits the researcher found it was the security guard who approached her; although it was done in a friendly way, it was off-putting.

The room used by the Women into Management course was on the first floor. It acted as a base room, had some computers and a place to leave coats, plus coffee and tea making facilities. The lavatory just along the corridor was a staff one so that all the students were issued with keys.

Students

As indicated above, this was a relatively well-qualified group of students. They had done a wide range of jobs, mainly white-collar and professional. Their partners were in middle-class employment and this was on the whole a middle-class group. Their style of dress indicated both a certain level of prosperity and aspirations to management positions. The ethnic spread was limited, with only one Asian woman and another who described herself as Asian/Irish. Their expectations of the course were instrumental – they either wanted to own their own businesses or to gain employment as a manager. Several women were having an enforced career break because of children and wanted to use the time productively.

Content of the course

The course was divided up into seven components:

• management
• computers
• interpersonal and professional skills
• project work
• finance
• career and life planning
• communications.

In addition, there were individual tutorials and a work placement. There was a session in the morning from 9.30 to 12.30 and one in the afternoon between 1.30 and 4.30. One topic would occupy each session. Computing was the only subject which had two slots a week. Quite a lot of the individual tutorial time was taken up with career planning. Students had to give feedback to the others at the end of their work placement. The organization of the work placement was very time consuming, with the consequence that individual tutorial time suffered. It was thought that visits to work situations might be preferable to long work placements.

Methodology

For most of the tutors there was an emphasis on group work and experiential learning in the way they presented their material. This was met by resistance from the students and gave rise to some problems. What tutors perceived as suitable methodology was not perceived in that way by the students. The question arose of whether tutors imposed their will or adapted their styles to fit the students' perceived needs. Other tutors met similar resistance, although the students were happier with some components of the course because they were more 'taught'. This raised problems for one tutor who thought she was 'overteaching' her component but felt that she needed to adopt that style to compensate for little formal input elsewhere.

Altogether the issue of methodology was a difficult one. It tied in with other issues like the recruitment and selection processes and the formation of the group dynamic. In the questionnaire at the end of the course it was interesting to see how highly the students rated the group experience – several mentioning it as the part of the course they enjoyed most.

Progression

By the end of the course only two or three had found work and then not in a management position. One woman intended to go into HE; two others were waiting until their children were older. One woman did not complete the course because of problems with child care. On the whole the course progression rate was not good. This may have tied in with the excellent child care on the course that could not be replicated afterwards. Some of the women's expectations were unrealistic and they had not thought through the consequences of moving into full-time employment with preschool or school age children.

Assessment and evaluation

The course was not externally assessed or validated but the women got a certificate of completion at the end. This may relate to methodology in that the women tended to dismiss feedback from their peers and preferred it to come from the tutors. There was an intention to get the course externally validated but it would have meant substantial changes.

There was a strong element of evaluation as the course progressed. The students' reactions and expressed needs were taken on board to some extent by the course team and, although this was not a comfortable experience, a negotiated outcome was reached.

What lessons can be learned from this case study?

1. The child care provision was a very important factor, extending as it did from preschool children to child care for two hours after school for school age children.
2. The negotiation about content and styles of presentation that went on during the course were important. Although this was not satisfactorily resolved, attempts were made to take note of students' comments and respond appropriately.
3. Course team meetings were a very important element and an example of good practice.
4. The levels of experience and education of the trainee at the start of the course needed to be more closely matched to the likely job prospects at the end; this means that a clear understanding of the aims and objectives of the course are needed with plenty of time for interviews.
5. Good facilities for women returners – a base room, toilet facilities, mature students' common room etc. – are important.
6. Developmental time for staff is needed and therefore a budget for this must be included.
7. Above all this case study demonstrates the need for careful and considered planning. This must include a clarity of purpose, a structuring of the curriculum and continuity between the stages of planning, recruitment and delivery.

Case study 6: A women's technology centre

This women's technology centre was housed in a modern office block in the city council's new technology centre. The WTC occupied part of the first floor and consisted of a large open-plan office area divided up by screens into comfortably sized working areas. The instructors had offices alongside this area, with windows overlooking it. The offices were shared and had desks, filing cabinets and a phone. The centre manager had her own office. There was one common room for staff and one for students. Altogether the work environment was relatively comfortable.

The original idea for the provision of a women-only technology centre came about from a visit to a similar centre in a nearby city. The idea was supported by the local Employment Initiative and a feasibility study was carried out. By 1986 the WTC was established and presented a 28 week course, later extended to 40 weeks. At the time of the research, the centre offered a variety of other courses, some to all-women groups and some to mixed groups.

The course

The course studied was for 35 weeks, running from January to December, with a break for school holidays and a work placement in September and

October. It ran from 9.30 to 2.30 each day. At the beginning of the course there was an induction period that included work on personal skills as well as the tasters. Having had taster sessions in this induction period, the women chose to concentrate on either electronics, programming or computing. They also did three hours a week on communications, life skills and business studies. The women on the computing option took at least four units of relevant City and Guilds (C&G) modules with the option of two more; those on the electronics option took five C&G units, and then had a number of options to choose from. The women on the programming course took three C&G modules. All the courses, therefore, had a modular structure, with each module taking approximately five weeks to complete. There were regular feedback sessions as each module was completed.

The course normally enrolled up to 40 trainees, although during the research period, two got jobs and one left because of childminding difficulties. The fact that the playgroup was in a separate building was seen as an advantage rather than a disadvantage, even though the trainees were responsible for their children during the lunch hour. There was no charge for the use of the playgroup and there was no fee for the course. The trainees received an attendance allowance and travel expenses. If they could not use the playgroup, they received a contribution towards childminding fees.

Aims and objectives

The aim of the computing, programming and electronics courses was to offer the trainees a stepping-stone to other training or employment and to provide them with basic vocational skills, leading to nationally recognized qualifications.

Publicity and recruitment

Leaflets were distributed to libraries, community groups, local colleges etc. More importantly, these places were visited to encourage potential trainees to find out more. An important method of publicity had been to distribute leaflets to former trainees and ask them to pass them on to their friends. Of 30 women who responded to a questionnaire, 20 gave 'word of mouth' as the means by which they heard of the course. Newspaper advertisements were the next most important source. There was also an 'open day' which was publicized locally and advertisements on local radio. Because of the name of the centre, the women-only nature of the provision was obvious in the publicity. In the general leaflet there were sections in two Asian languages. Initial demand for the course was high and there seemed to be no difficulty filling places. Women were interviewed for a place in threes or fours; this was a great asset as many would not have come through the door without a friend. Although there was theoretically open access, trainees did have to have basic numeracy and literacy. There was a brief numeracy test for the electronics option.

Reception and registration

The centre was modern, cheerful and welcoming. There were clear signs in the foyer, indicating that the WTC was on the first floor, served by stairs and a lift. At the top of the stairs there was a large welcoming display of photographs of women of different ethnic origins using the equipment. There was a clearly labelled reception area. The trainees had to log themselves in and out of the centre and a check was kept on attendance.

Trainees

The trainees at WTC were usually women who left school at 16 with few or no qualifications. They had, on the whole, done low paid jobs between leaving school and coming on the course. If living with a partner, the partner was usually of working-class occupation. There was a wide ethnic spread with Asian, Afro-Caribbean and white women. In the main, they saw the course as providing them with qualifications and, hopefully, with jobs.

Content of the courses

Depending on the option concerned, the trainees took units in:

word processing
database methods
spreadsheet methods
coding and programming in BASIC
computers and computing
electronic circuits and components
digital electronics
introductory microprocessors
microcomputer technology.

Whatever option they were taking, the trainees all undertook supplementary training which included communication skills, literacy skills, presentation techniques, interview and job seeking skills. There was also a work placement for four weeks, with a feedback session afterwards.

Methodology

Because of the nature of the training – much of it consisted of an individual woman using a piece of equipment or a computer – it was to some extent difficult to use group processes. There was a marked emphasis on learning by doing. A typical session would consist of a trainer giving a short explanation or demonstration, using either the equipment or a flip chart, and then setting the students a task, usually on a handout. The students then worked through the task but called on each other or the tutor for help. This developed a cooperative spirit among the trainees and a good working relationship between trainees and trainer. On the whole trainers remained pleasant, cheerful and helpful. There was an obvious advantage in this short exposition/demonstration, then 'have a go and shout if stuck' approach with mixed ability groups as it allowed those who were able to get on with it, thus freeing the trainer to help those who were stuck. When interviewed about their methodology several of the trainers emphasized the importance of breaking down the barriers between trainer and trainee and consciously worked towards this by demystifying language and acknowledging that each relationship was different. There was a sense in which the trainers were just trying to share their knowledge. The emphasis was very much on pointing out the good things, making women feel their contribution was valid and encouraging women to work together.

Progression

In the past the trainees had gone on to a wide variety of jobs and courses; it was estimated that 90 per cent of the women did this. In the future the centre was to be increasingly concerned in identifying the skills gaps in the local market to make sure that trainees were given every chance to take up those jobs or gain further skills training.

Assessment and evaluation

The course units were assessed against the external criteria of City and Guilds or RSA. The assessments took place at the centre when the trainee was ready for it. If by chance she did not do well enough, she could always try again. Thus assessment was carried out in a positive way. In addition the WTC issued two certificates of its own, one when a course was completed and the other showing the subjects taken and the grades achieved. Despite great sensitivity and care there could have been a problem if a trainee was left behind, but the staff supported her and helped her catch up.

What particular lessons can be learned from this case study?

1. The publicity material was of a high quality – lots of photos showing women of different ethnic groups – and presented in community languages as well as English.
2. The course administrator and one of the trainers were black women; the trainer herself had completed a course at the centre.
3. The course led in a structured way to nationally recognized qualifications.

4. The teaching style took account of the women-only nature of the provision within a typically male area of work. Conscious attempts were made to demystify what was being learned, to build on what was already known and to foster cooperation.
5. This teaching style was particularly appropriate for mixed ability groups.
6. There was concern about providing women with low levels of qualification in male dominated spheres of work. The implications of this were recognized and ways forward sought.

These six case studies of different kinds of women-only provision provide a lot of information about their curricula and raise several specific issues which need further exploration. The next chapter looks at six main issues in some depth.

7 | The Curriculum of Women-only Provision – The Main Themes

After several months visiting and observing the case study provision (described in the previous chapter and Coats *et al.* 1988), certain common themes began to emerge, namely the influence of ideology, the importance of inspiration and motivation, the concept of ownership, the significance of group dynamics, the role of assessment, and the need for progression.

Ideology

Most educational provision for women is governed by several interrelated ideologies (i.e. frameworks of ideas and ideals which inform policy and practice). Some of these ideologies are explicitly stated; others are implicit but evident. Within any one type of provision, one ideology may dominate or a range of various, possibly conflicting, ideologies may coexist. The ideologies which inform policy may not be those which guide practice.

In each of the six case studies, the influence of ideologies was clear and it was possible to identify a range of them, since different ideological frameworks can be translated into various kinds of feminist educational provision (see Chapter 3 for a fuller discussion of this).

Ideology in the case studies

Four of the studies had an ideology which could be described as feminist – broadly liberal but with some individuals demonstrating a more radical feminist or socialist feminist approach. By far the most common was an intention to provide educational opportunities which would redress and reduce inequality for women – whether inequality as women or inequality as working-class women. The feminist emphasis varied. All were open about the 'for women' nature of their provision but, for the two daytime short courses, this is accepted as appropriate, since daytime classes with a crèche are expected to attract only women. All advertised their provision as 'for women' and not as women only (i.e. no men). Linked to this was a strong compensatory educational emphasis – giving women a 'second chance'. Whilst neither short course utilized traditional educational methods, attitudes to mainstream education were mixed. Most tutors realized that if women were to have a reasonable chance of fulfilling their potential, gaining independence and succeeding in the world of paid work, then they needed to enter and successfully complete courses in higher education or further vocational training. All these studies saw the main route to success as being via education (but see section on progression later).

The NOW course, as the title implies, was for women only but this was not emphasized, just accepted. Both tutors shared feminist perspectives, one possibly more 'radical' and more overtly socialist than the other. But both were careful not to present a 'women's lib.' image in case it alienated women. The overall emphasis of the course was on individual personal reorientation and growth but within a group situation. There was little educational skills work as such but intensive input on personal reassessment and possible progression routes – educational, vocational training or directly into work. It was seen as compensatory to a certain extent but all women were accepted regardless of previous qualifications/experience if it was thought appropriate for them.

The WEA Return to Learn courses had been described by its tutors as 'socialist feminist' but this was not made overt; it was advertised as a 'free course for women'. The tutors varied in the emphasis placed on 'feminist' issues but all expressed concern that it should not be threatening to the women.

The educational emphasis seemed to be 'compensatory' and aimed to facilitate women's return to education. Progression was through various types of provision if desired and the focus was definitely on education and not training. The methodology reflected the need for confidence enhancing as well as basic skills; some literacy and numeracy problems were identified.

Tutors at the residential college were very conscious of a possible gap between stated and intended ideology and current practice. This was made more complex by the fact that there were ten members of the teaching staff and there were differences in opinion and practice. Most would accept a compensatory educational aim and wished to provide a route to higher education. Others would have more diverse aims. Some were overtly feminist but liberal rather than radical (there were three male tutors).

One difference which emerged over implementation was the extent of coercion and control. On the one hand there was a feeling that this was full-time funded provision and students should, for example, be expected to fulfil certain requirements. On the other hand there was a feeling that these were adult women who must be responsible for their own learning. Equally, since most proceed to higher education, some felt that academic standards should be rigorous so that women were prepared for the traditional world of higher education; others felt that these conventions should be challenged.

All stages in the conception, development and delivery of the Access course were informed to varying degrees, by an explicit feminist ideology. The course had its roots in women's groups which grew out of the 1984–6 miners' strike. The original proposal was taken to the college by a tutor who was very much involved in women's studies. The course was developed under an Equal Opportunities banner and was coordinated by a tutor who has an explicit feminist approach. Although students may have been initially disturbed by this, it seemed that many of them were relieved to be presented with a view of the world with which they could identify and which became the source of their new found confidence. All aspects of the course were delivered from a woman's point of view and this seemed to become increasingly important for the women on the course.

All four studies, whatever their educational emphasis, saw individual confidence enhancement and personal growth as primary aims. None of them showed overt signs of encouraging women to work collectively towards challenging patriarchy.

The other two studies demonstrated a wider range of ideological frameworks – both between the two studies and the four previously described, and, in some cases, within the studies themselves. Different tutors had different starting points and not all were informed by feminist ideology, or the need, even, to run women-only courses.

For all the tutors except one on the Women into Management course there was an underlying feminist ideology. The tutor who did not share this view had recently entered further education from business and she saw herself, and the students saw her, as being more in tune with the students' needs than the other tutors. The women on the course were not particularly attracted in the first place by the women-onlyness, nor were some of them concerned that it should be women-only, even when on the course. Their concern was with the content (management) rather than the way it was provided (in a women-only environment), although the provision of child care facilities was seen as being of crucial importance by a substantial number of them. This raised interesting questions, both about ideological differences within the tutor group, and between the majority of the tutors and the students. There were implications here for the recruitment both of staff and students and also for progression, as most of these women were hoping to gain employment in a largely male-dominated sector.

A further dimension of the issue of ideology is brought out by the Women's Technology Centre. The emphasis here was on training women to have skills which they could then use, more or less immediately, in the workplace. That is not to say that the issue of women-onlyness was ignored – it certainly was not. For some women, Muslim trainees for example, the fact that it was for women only was crucial; they would not otherwise have been able to attend. The emphasis placed on women-only provision by the trainers was variable. Some were very clear about it and had consciously adapted their teaching styles to fit in with this; others placed less value on it. There was, however, an increasing awareness of the issues around progression and an increasing concern that the centre should be doing more than preparing women for low-paid employment.

Inspiration and motivation

In the same way that ownership emerged as a theme during the course of the research, the combined issue of inspiration and motivation came out of the case studies. It became apparent that the courses had been initiated for very different reasons, ranging from initiatives from women themselves to institutional initiatives and in some cases, decisions made by city councils. It was interesting to consider the effect this had on the nature and permanence of the provision. This is a theme that has special relevance in the light of the changing demands of the labour market and of the need to ensure that the progress made in women's education is not just a response to current economic requirements but becomes part of mainstream educational provision.

Of all the six themes this was probably the most difficult to disentangle and identify. It is closely linked with ideology. On most of the courses the overall inspiration was the perceived and accepted need to provide educational opportunities for women, to redress their educational and social disadvantage.

Inspiration and motivation in the case studies

The NOW course was located in a college with a long tradition of provision for women and for other disadvantaged groups in the community, thus the motivation for initiating and maintaining the course came from that commitment and various courses for women were well established in the college. The WEA RTL provision was less secure. In the WEA nationally, the provision of women-only courses came after a long struggle to establish the need. We should not assume that once established, however, such provision is totally accepted. There is always a need to argue and defend work which, by its short-term nature, is vulnerable to cuts.

The residential college's motivation is rooted in its past tradition of providing an educational opportunity for women who have missed out earlier. While this compensatory motivation is still strong, other issues such as which women should be provided for and what form this provision should take have to be debated. Even in a climate of expanding access for adults, the importance of residential provision and for women-only provision still needs to be argued.

The access course was a consequence of two sources of inspiration. On the one hand there was the initiative from women's groups which had grown out of the 1984 miners' strike; on the other hand there was the commitment of a local college of further education to equality of opportunity. The strength of the provision derived in part from the combination of the demands of the particular group of women and an institution which was sensitive to and supportive of their needs.

With the Women into Management course the history was more complex. The Economic Development Unit of the city council had asked the college to provide the course. One reason was the college's known expertise; the other was that a lecturer there had been a student on a management course for women. There were educational and political reasons for wanting to have a course in the city, and economic reasons in that European Social Fund (ESF) funding had already been sought.

The initiation of the WTC can also be partly explained in political terms in that it was part of the council's employment initiative. Research into other centres was carried out and a feasibility study was done in 1983, after which a proposal was submitted and the centre opened in 1985. Political changes following the local elections in October 1988 could have resulted in difficulties for the centre but at the time of the research project the future seemed assured, provided that economic use was made of the provision. This meant that the centre would have to be used for mixed groups at other times of the day, but it seemed likely that the 35 week, full-time provision for women would continue. Of all the studies this is the one which had to operate most obviously within financial constraints and it is apparent that a close watch was being kept on its financial viability.

Ownership

At the beginning of the research into these six case studies of women-only provision it seemed likely that some issues would emerge as more important than others. The significance of the group process, for example, was not a surprise. However, as the research went on, other issues which were not anticipated began to emerge. One of these was 'ownership' by the providers. This refers to the ownership of the process, or the various stages in the process, from the original idea for the course, through the submission of the bid to gain whatever funding was necessary, to the development and delivery of the course. There was a range in the studies from those where that process belonged to one person or group of people, to those where the different stages were the responsibility of different people and where, in some cases, the transition from one person to another had not been a smooth one. As the research progressed it seemed that the continuity or otherwise in that process had marked effects on the outcome and so the issue of ownership came to be one of the main themes.

Ownership in the case studies

The issue was not particularly problematic in either the NOW course or the RTL provision. Although some of the women originally responsible for designing the provision were no longer involved, the current tutors continued to develop the courses. This was not to suggest that all the changes were free from controversy but that the current 'owners' saw themselves as responsible for the current provision. Neither course was stagnant nor bound by older traditions. All the tutors had a degree of autonomy in how they interpreted the overall aims and objectives and on what content they included in the class.

At the residential college there was a tradition of compensatory provision for women who had missed out on their education. Whilst not rejecting this tradition, there had been a change in the nature of the provision – to focus on those women most disadvantaged by previous schooling or other circumstances, especially working-class and black women. There had been major changes in the content of the course, in its modular presentation and in the length of the course.

With a large staff, some of whom had been at the college for a considerable time, it was inevitable that changes would cause concern. What was evident is that such changes, and differences in opinion about them, were openly acknowledged and discussed, thus any conflict or contention was more likely to lead to an acceptance of change. Such controversy was not comfortable and yet was possibly the key to successful change. Unless differences of opinion were acknowledged and worked through, no workable consensus could emerge. This reflected a style of management which allowed such differences to emerge.

The access course was an interesting example of mixed ownership. The course had its roots in the women's groups which grew up in the 1984 miners' strikes; it was fostered by a vice-principal who appointed a member of staff to develop it and it was then coordinated by another member of staff from outside the college. However, the consequences of this mixed ownership were not disruptive. There had been some minor modifications in how the course was presented and to its content, but on the whole, it served the group of women it set out to serve and did what it set out to do. It may be that its success in this was related to the context of the provision. Although different groups and people had a hand in developing and delivering the course it was set in the context of a further education college committed to developing equal opportunities so that although the agents had changed, the underlying structure remained. In this case, management ensured that the emphasis was on continuity rather than change.

The Women into Management course was another example of the importance of ownership and, in this case, the effect on course construction and recruitment. The course came to the college as a result of a decision by the city council. The go-ahead for the course was given relatively late in the academic year, prior to its start in the autumn and the developmental work was carried out by two consultants who were outside of the college and then, not without some disruption, passed to an internal member of staff to coordinate. The coordinator was a woman committed to providing women's courses who took over at relatively short notice. She had the task of recruiting and interviewing students, without having as much information on the nature and intent of the course as would have been the case if she had been involved fully from the beginning. Consequently there was a mismatch between the students' expectations and what the course was offering. This demonstrated the difficulties which can arise from different ownership at different stages.

Ownership and continuity were key issues at the WTC. The council and the European Social Fund (ESF) jointly provided the funding. The original idea had come from another nearby women's training scheme and the first coordinator carried on this feminist tradition. Things changed with the appointment of the next coordinator, which coincided with the changing economic and local political climate, described earlier. During the course of the research, a third coordinator was appointed and the issue of changing ownership continued. However, the question of ownership and continuity is not simply one of replacing people but must be located in changing ideologies, both personal and political.

As these case studies show, it is the management of change in ownership and the consequent effect on continuity which is crucial. Where the underlying ideology remains consistent, then changes in personnel and content can be accommodated more comfortably.

Group dynamics

It has been suggested earlier that women's education has been significantly influenced by the politics and practices of the Women's Liberation Movement. In the 1970s women's groups frequently engaged in 'consciousness raising' sessions where individual women were given space to share their feelings and were encouraged and supported by other women in the group. Many women's classes have used a group as a medium for sharing problems and supporting its members in this way. Some courses have included sessions of group counselling, assertiveness training and problem sharing as part of their programme.

Given the isolation of women in the home and the lack of confidence felt by many women after years of child rearing and domestic duties, the dynamics of the group have proved an important part of many reorientation courses. Discovering that other women shared feelings of inferiority, guilt or worthlessnes enabled women to realize that the problem was not peculiar to them and that they were not to 'blame'. Thus they were able to locate their experience in a wider social context.

The group, too, acts as a support for individual women. Re-entry to education is often accompanied by change – a change in external circumstances (e.g. youngest child starting school; the end of a marriage) and/or a change within the woman herself (e.g. wanting a new direction in life; needing stimulation; coping with loneliness). Thus the group can support a woman as she comes to terms with what can be painful changes. The group can share, too, the implications of returning to education in the other areas of a woman's life. In all women's education, no matter what the content or level, the existence of the group and the dynamics within it are important. The creation of a group identity and the close relationships in it, however, has serious consequences for progression, and this will be taken up in a later section.

In any group of women, one issue that cannot be ignored is the effects of the diversity of the women in a group – differences in age and educational attainment, differences based on social class or racial origin. We cannot assume that just because all the members of the group are women that they will share interests and outlook or that there will be mutual understanding and support. Tolerance of difference has to be encouraged and it is easy for less articulate or less confident women to feel insecure; it is easy for some women to feel that their experiences are not relevant and their interests not catered for. Skilled tutors recognize this and allow the differences to be recognized and valued. Mutual support between women across social divisions is possible but it is not automatic. Many privileged or more gifted women do not realize their ability to oppress other women, particularly if they are concerned with their own problems.

Group dynamics in the case studies

Various factors affected group dynamics – size of the group, frequency of meeting, perceptions, intentions and skills of the tutors – but the interrelationship of the variables is complex. NOW students met for only one day a week for 10–12 weeks and yet the group dynamics were possibly the most important part of this provision. This was because the two tutors concerned placed great emphasis on group identity and it appeared high in their aims for the course:

> Aim 1: To build a secure and cohesive group of local women where issues, concerns and ideas can be shared in an atmosphere of openness, trust and support.

This aim was achieved because both tutors were skilled in group work and because they had the personal qualities of effective group facilitators. Right from the start of the course a series of 'ice breakers' and self-concept exercises carried out in the group quickly established a non-threatening environment and positive relationships within it. Careful pairing and subgrouping ensured that all the women knew each other and prevented cliques forming or dominant individuals emerging. In group sessions contributions from all women were valued and guidelines for good group interaction were devised by the group for the group. One session each week focused on personal development but within a group context. Each session began with a sharing experience which deliberately reinforced group cohesion. In the women's studies component of the course the focus on childhood, marriage and family allowed women to share and to value their own experiences and opinions. One of the most impressive results of this group work was that the women, who were from very different backgrounds, managed to find common experiences and support for each other.

In the three NOW courses covered during the year this approach was very successful and a very supportive group emerged in each one. There are both advantages and disadvantages in this. The support of the group and the friendships forged within it were clearly very important for most of the women in the group but the less regular attenders may have felt a bit on the fringe.

Most women from each course wanted to continue with some further study or course but wanted to do it together; this is clearly a problem. Others who tried courses on their own found it difficult without the support of the group, although several were apparently doing well. Progression was taken very seriously by the tutors and there was a lot of personal and group information and advice. The danger was that some of the weaker women may have become too dependent on the group and had to be 'weaned'. (See the discussion on progression later in this chapter.)

Similar activities took place in the WEA 'Return to Learn' (RTL) courses where group support was very evident. However the time available (two hours a week) and the RTL focus of the provision meant that group cohesion was more difficult to achieve and that the emphasis was on shared learning experiences rather than on personal issues. This too provided support and encouragement for individual women and was the principal medium for the rediscovery and recognition of skills. Similarly, guidelines for group behaviour were established by the women and implemented by skilled tutors. Group activities were an important part of the methodology and the use of the group as a resource and for support was intentional. Given the short time available and different skills and styles of tutors, this cohesion was achieved very successfully.

Although there was greater homogeneity in these groups, which catered for working-class women having minimal educational qualifications, each class did contain one or more black women in it. In this provision there was a strong commitment to raising issues of equal opportunities and to challenging overt racism. However, there was a problem in some groups over class issues. Although all the women had few or no qualifications and most had done only unskilled work, some projected a more 'middle-class' image than others (e.g. articulate, more confident, apparently more informed). This could have intimidated the more obviously disadvantaged women and these were the ones who did not complete the course. To create a supportive group identity under these conditions requires considerable skill and sensitivity. The NOW courses attracted only white women but from all social classes and educational backgrounds. Even with this considerable diversity, however, mutually supportive links were made and group coherence was strong.

Both the NOW and the WEA RTL provision had components in the curriculum where individual performance was necessary and this could have affected the group coherence. In the NOW computing sessions and in the maths RTL courses, some activities had to be individually performed. These individual elements were not divisive or competitive because other opportunities were used to create and reinforce group identity and shared learning. However, if no such opportunity is made available and there is no ethos of sharing and supporting, individual skill based courses would have to consider how group dynamics operate.

The long-term residential college was different in that the number of women involved and the wide range of courses offered meant that smaller groupings were not so easy to identify. Of all the case studies this was the most difficult to analyse in terms of group dynamics. Certainly there was group solidarity and support – a large number of women living together and sharing sometimes stressful experiences made this inevitable. But it was more difficult to work out just which groups operated well and how they did this. First there were residents and day students – that made a difference – but within the residents there were other groupings, one of which was radical feminist in nature. Then there were tutor groups – all were assigned a personal tutor. Although these groups met, they did not necessarily have much in common or form close support units (tutors supported individual students but group processes did not seem very strong). Then there were groups based on the same module choice; the choices for the first semester were significant since those women shared the same demands (for essays etc.) and, through supporting each other, formed enduring relationships. Then there were certain students who were taking the social work option and these formed a group, deliberately encouraged by the tutor responsible for this course. So the picture was complex – but with 70 women students this may be inevitable. What was evident at this college was that the same commitment to supportive, non-competitive, shared learning did exist, whilst allowing for the progression of individual women. To enable this to happen required sensitivity and skill on the part of the tutors.

The whole development, content and delivery of the access course was overtly feminist and so the idea of group support and the emphasis on group work and cooperation was inherent. For many of the students on this course the move into education was a large step to take and, for some, it was a step taken without the support of their families. The role of the group in terms of providing support through this change was very important and all of the tutors seemed to be aware of this in their teaching. The expressed importance placed on it by the students changed throughout the year. At the beginning its relevance was acknowledged; by the end it had become of paramount importance. This may have been helped by the relative homogeneity of the group – all except one of the students were white and all were working-class women who, on the whole, had lived most of their lives in the area. The part that the initial counselling and selection process had to play has to be acknowledged as, on the whole, it was working-class women who had not benefited from their earlier encounters with the education system who were selected to join the course. After early drop-outs (one unavoidable in that the woman concerned had no option but to join the Employment Training Scheme) the group remained constant in size and the fact that this was a full-time 36 week course played a part in the development of the group identity.

The process of the formation of group identity was more problematic in the Women into Management course. Although only 14 weeks in length, it was a full-time course and most of the tutors placed a great deal of emphasis on building up good group relationships. Their teaching material was, on the whole, devised with that in mind – experiential learning, worksheets, learning from each other etc. The students' perceptions were, however, slightly different to those of the staff; they were to some extent resistant to methods which drew on the group's experience and some expressed a preference for a more traditional didactic mode of teaching and learning. Additionally, some tensions developed within the group; some felt that cliques were formed and that consequently some of the less articulate women were not able to express their needs. There was also a racial dimension to these tensions and so the whole issue of group dynamics was complex.

Some of these issues were taken up by the course coordinator and her colleagues and were, to some extent, resolved. A group identity was established – for example the women met after the end of the course – but it was not a smooth process. There were perhaps links here to the process of recruitment and selection and to the need for continuity in the stages of initiation, development and delivery of a course.

At WTC there seemed to be less emphasis on the development of group dynamics. There was some group work during the introductory period and although some women said they found this rather threatening at the time, they did agree afterwards that it had been worth doing. The extent to which group processes were then emphasized depended on the trainer and also on the area of training – coming to terms with a word processing system can be perhaps a more individual experience than becoming acquainted with the intricacies of electronics. It is probably true to say, however, that some of the staff who had been appointed to the centre when it was first set up were more committed to the idea of the 'group' than were those appointed later. Within the trainee group there were some difficulties which were tied in with assessment (as discussed below) because trainees were looking towards City and Guilds and RSA qualifications. Some could proceed at a faster rate than others. This could have been a problem for those who saw themselves as 'left behind', and this had implications for group cohesion.

Assessment

If women's education challenges traditional education on issues of content and methodology, then the place of assessment is even more problematic. If the content places emphasis and value on personal experience, how can this be assessed in any formal sense? If the method of delivery uses cooperative, shared, non-competitive means, then assessment methods must recognize this. Traditional modes of assessment which are individualized and competitive are clearly counter-productive to the aims and objectives of most women's education.

There are three major arguments in support of student assessment:

1. Many women wanted feedback on their performance and wanted to know how well they had done. Even more significantly, women wanted that feedback to be honest – both good and bad. If a woman is re-entering education to compensate for previous failure, then the assessment of her efforts and her ability is important but possibly emotive and even painful.

How, when and for what purpose women re-entering education are assessed is a key issue.

2. In many of the case studies, women wanted to progress to mainstream education courses and so evaluation and assessment were important because the women (and the future providers) needed to know if they were ready and capable of further study. They might have needed to gain qualifications which were externally recognized.

3. Women needed to experience being assessed. Submitting a piece of work for assessment or taking an examination was an important learning experience. Again, it was how, when and why it was done that were the main issues.

From these studies it can be seen that the issue of assessment was tied in closely with guidance and support. Potentially the process of assessment can be stressful and counter-productive to confidence enhancement, which is the core of women-only provision. For those who are vulnerable the difficulties can be overcome by sensitive and well thought out support and by encouraging women to see that their possible lack of attainment may not be a personal failure but reflects a system which has disadvantaged them. For those who are successful, the attainment of recognized qualifications can not only boost confidence and self-esteem but also open the way to more advanced courses or to employment.

Assessment in the case studies

NOW had no assessment at all. The tutors had decided not to go for open college federation validation although other women's studies courses at the college were part of the scheme. The very 'personal' nature of their provision and the flexibility they enjoyed might have been threatened by validation. One of the main strengths of this provision was that the tutors could adapt, create or change courses to suit the needs of the particular group – and to prevent themselves becoming stale. Validation would have restricted this flexibility. However, some of the women on the NOW course also took or intended to take, courses that were externally validated.

On the WEA RTL courses no formal assessment of students was made but a certificate of attendance was given. There was an ongoing discussion amongst the tutors about the importance of individual 'project' work. (This discussion was included under assessment because it had a hidden dimension of competition and achievement, i.e. who completed it; who did a 'good' project.) There was some concern that this was too threatening and may have caused women to stop coming, so there was a change to producing a class magazine rather than individual projects. The important thing was the awareness of tutors about this and the level of analysis and discussion in tutors' meetings about it.

If assessment did not play a part on these two short courses, at the long-term college it was a major issue. This is because the courses were validated and accepted as an alternative qualification for entry to higher education. Originally the two year course was validated by the CNAA, but this had been reduced to a one year validated course. Although women could stay two years, it was for those who demonstrated that they needed the two year course, and not for the majority. Most women were able to obtain the CNAA certificate in one year and some higher education institutions were even willing to exempt such women from the first year of a degree course.

However, most women accepted by this college had no formal qualifications and started from a very basic academic level – thus the task of reaching CNAA-validated standards was considerable. There was no assessment for the first five weeks but after that work was assessed and counted towards the final result. The tutors had to get students inducted into the college, develop the necessary study skills, build up confidence – and produce work for assessment. In addition to this, much of the academic work was traditional in both content and method – set syllabus and essays, with end of module exams.

The sense of panic engendered by the first assessed essay was considerable and the women had to be supported through this experience, but by the end of the year the same women were facing examinations with confidence. Almost all the women successfully gained the certificate and for those that did not, and for the few with acute learning problems, there was extra help and support. The follow-up on women who proceeded to other institutions of higher education – both universities and polytechnics – showed that they had been well prepared.

Despite the difficulty which some people see over providing a course which leads to a final qualification, this did seem to be one of the strengths of the access course. The fact that the course was externally validated and could provide access into further and higher education was valued by the women and helped to improve their confidence. However it is important to realize that the assessment and qualifications issue has to be seen in the context of support and guidance. Working towards qualifications and feminist educational practice are not mutually exclusive as long as that practice is fully supportive of women in the assessment process.

The Women into Management course had no external assessment, although individual tutorials took place to assess progress and there were internal informal assessments of students' work. For some women, but not all, the fact that there was no external qualification was a problem, but in terms of their own assessment of the course, most of the women spoke positively of the benefits gained. There were, however, other issues concerned with assessment which lay both in the group processes and with the ownership of the course. The group was keen to have more formal feedback from the tutors about their work and were reticent about accepting feedback from other members of the group. It may have been the case that if the course had been developed and delivered by the same people, i.e. if the ownership had been the same from start to finish, that the issue of assessment and qualifications would have turned out differently.

The issues of assessment and qualifications were more straightforward at the WTC. The women were there to be trained and the measure of success was the City and Guilds and RSA qualifications which they received. However, this could cause problems, as mentioned earlier. Some women acquired qualifications more quickly than others and this could lead to a sense of failure or, at the very least, a sense of inequality of ability. However, this was treated sensitively by the tutors; trainees were given extra help and extra time to 'catch up' so that on the whole every trainee finished the year with some qualifications.

Progression

All the case studies participating in the project shared one thing in common; they provided opportunities for women at the point of re-entry to education or training. Indeed, this is one of the major arguments for women-only provision and one of the categories under which it can be legally offered. Women-only provision like this has been criticized, however, if it does not enable women to progress to further educational or training opportunities, or does not equip women for suitable paid employment. If the arguments for women-only provision are to be justified then the appropriate progression of the women must be seen as one indicator of success.

For most of the women progression would be into mixed provision – education, training or employment. Their women-only experiences should not be so supportive that they are unable to survive in a male dominated environment and they need to be equipped for this. Some would go further and argue that they should be equipped to question that dominance and challenge any sexist or racist practice they encounter. Some of the tutors did, if practicable, continue to support women as they moved on, if that is what the women required.

There was a strong emphasis on progression in all the case studies; all tried to provide adequate information and counselling on what options were available and what each woman felt was appropriate for her needs. Providers wondered if they had failed if a woman slipped away without advice, back into the same circumstances as before. Raising expectations which cannot be fulfilled was another concern. Each study tried hard to remove the barriers of finance, child care, inaccessibility etc., but these same barriers may prevent women moving on to another provider who is less sensitive to their needs.

When women made their choices after knowing what was possible, this was respected. For some it was essential to take any employment offered, during or after the course; for others it may have been right to return to full-time domestic duties for the immediate future. So progression and its use to evaluate provision has to be understood in the personal and social context of individual women and not simply as a statistical exercise.

Progression in the case studies

Most of the courses took progression very seriously and provided both information about options and individual counselling to help women decide what to do next. The NOW course was in the fortunate position of being located in a college which offered a range of suitable courses after NOW. There was a possibility of continuing on a NOW Two course if sufficient women were interested. There were several other women-only courses, various 'open learning' options, all the usual GCSE and BTEC choices and a validated access course.

Most women from NOW, except those who found employment, continued with something offered by the college. The timing of the courses was relevant here since those who took the autumn term course had two more terms of supported learning before having to decide on their next major step. Spring term women had one term of NOW Two or other provision and only the summer term women had to make more immediate choices before the next college year started in the following September. Another major advantage of the provision was that it was served by an excellent education and guidance service whose staff contributed to the course and whose offices nearby were always accessible for individual women.

The options open to women from the WEA RTL courses were probably wider for women than anywhere outside of London and one of the stated aims of the course was to help women decide what to go on to next. RTL provided an excellent preparation for 'second chance' courses, access courses or any other full or part-time provision in the area. A diagrammatic map of the local provision used in one of the sessions showed graphically what was available and where women could go for further information and advice. While some women were constrained by their circumstances (finance, family responsibilities, lack of mobility etc.) there was something appropriate for most women should they wish, as most did, to continue. There were also women-only training schemes available.

Although most women from the RTL courses looked towards more educational options, all were encouraged to make their own choices, which could include postponing further study or taking paid employment. Both courses found there were women who needed more help with basic skills or ESL provision, although there was a problem of timing since shorter courses started at different times in the year and so gaps between options were possible. For women who had got themselves and their families into a routine that allowed for their studying, a break could prove a barrier to progress.

What was not so easy for tutors on this kind of course was to advise women who clearly had psychological problems or who were rehabilitating themselves after treatment. Quite significant numbers of women who have been damaged by the emotional and social pressures in their family or wider society look to education as a way of recovery. Women-only provision has helped many such women, but the problem of progression for them is often a cause for concern and requires skilled handling.

Progression at the residential college was part of its main function as this extract from their submission to the CNAA shows:

> It is primarily concerned to recruit women who have missed educational opportunities earlier in life and who now wish to clarify their own educational and vocational requirements through study and consider their options for the future. From the start of the course, the College emphasises the importance of helping students in the diagnosis of future needs.

This was done through career and educational planning sessions as part of the core studies taken by every student and through formal and informal personal counselling with tutors. One of the great advantages of a full-time course, particularly for residential students, was that there was sufficient time to make all the information available and to support women through the process of deciding on their next step.

The college stressed that its courses could lead to a variety of outcomes but the majority of its students proceeded to degree courses or to CQSW provision. Even women who entered with minimal educational qualifications and very unsatisfying past educational histories could, after one year, proceed to higher education and be successful.

The only major problem, again, is timing, in that UCCA and PCAS forms had to be completed just weeks after the start of the first term. The confusion and upheaval of the first few weeks, coupled with initial doubts about ability, was not the best time to be making decisions about their long-term future. Yet by the following autumn many women were ready to move on to higher education and did not need a second year of study. Some changes and late choices were possible but this seems to indicate a potential problem for many providers of access routes to higher education.

Each year ex-students who went on to higher education came back to the college to share with current students their experiences. All acknowledged the support and help they received there and most were fairly critical of conventional provision. All said they were well prepared in terms of both content and skills. So clearly the college was working – but conventional education is not changing. This is not just a matter of feminist practice but of all good adult education. Maybe increasing numbers of adults in higher education will challenge it.

Progression was an issue which was taken very seriously by the providers of the access course. It was one of the reasons why steps were taken to have the course accredited by the open college federation (OCF) because it was felt that women needed to have an externally recognized validation if they were to move on to higher education. The course provided access both to local universities and polytechnics; there was progression on to other universities and also on to other courses at the college. All of the women who wanted to move on to other courses or employment were able to do so. For the women themselves, the fact that they had fulfilled the requirements of an externally validated course was important, both in terms of 'allowing' them to go on to other courses and in giving them the confidence to do so.

The aim of the Women into Management course was to enable women to return to work and, to some extent it was successful. Some women did gain employment but not necessarily in the management field. Some were going on to higher education but the timing of the course was important here in that the course ran from October to February and so left a gap before the beginning of the next academic year. There was an additional problem identified by the course coordinator relating to the unrealistic expectations of some of the students. She felt that some had not assessed their position realistically and were reluctant to take on board what would be required of them to reach their desired goals. Other tutors felt that the students' expectations were informed by the course publicity and that students were not appropriately selected in the first place. This goes back to the need for continuity in the process, from course initiation to delivery, and also to the need for clarity in the publicity, interview and selection stages. The students themselves raised the question of the validity of a women-only course when the field in which they would be seeking employment would be dominated by men.

The link between qualifications and progression is well demonstrated by the WTC. This is a training centre where women were accredited by external qualifications and the intention was that those qualifications would be used to gain employment. At one level this was what happened, although some did go on to further or higher education. Increasingly questions were asked about the kind of work to which the women progressed and whether, in fact, it was possible to prepare them for better paid and higher status employment.

The exploration of these six themes in each of the case studies led to a series of recommendations and guidelines for good practice in women-only provision and to a framework of analysis which could be applied to all provision for women. These recommendations are discussed in the next chapter.

8 | The Curriculum of Women-only Provision – Recommendations and Guidelines

Introduction

One of the main aims of the research project described in the two previous chapters was to draw from the case studies examples of good practice and to provide guidelines for other organizations and institutions which want to improve their educational provision for women. Although the study focused on women-only provision and the recommendations and guidelines directly address this, many of the findings are applicable in a wider context. Many of the guidelines are relevant to all educational provision where women participate. If the curriculum of good women's education can be described as women-centred; this is very similar to student-centred provision in a specific context. The lessons from a good women-centred setting can enhance good student-centred provision. For example, these recommendations and guidelines can be related to aspects of further and higher education, particularly where providers are being challenged by increasing numbers of adult students. The recommendations and guidelines which follow have wider implications than provision for women only. The specific recommendations listed below need to be viewed in the context of the six emerging themes that have been described in the previous chapter. These themes can be summarized in the following manner.

Ideology

The ideology underlying the development and delivery of the courses has been shown to be a key issue throughout the research. It is therefore recommended that tutors be aware of the needs of women returners and can set the difficulties likely to be experienced by this group in an ideological context, enabling them to use the women's personal experiences as a way of understanding the structural context. It is not essential that tutors share identical views of the position of women in our society but that the ideological assumptions informing such views are exposed and acknowledged.

Inspiration and motivation

In a similar way the underlying reasons why a course is presented at all have practical repercussions and there is a need to keep the interests of the women, rather than those of the institution, uppermost.

Ownership

The continuity of ownership between the various stages in the process of devising and delivering a course for women has a number of practical implications. One of the conclusions from the research is that better provision results if there is continuity throughout that process. This does not mean that the people responsible for the course must not change but that any change of personnel must recognize the need for continuity of purpose and that any changes are openly negotiated and agreed.

Group dynamics

The dynamics in the group have been shown to affect both the experiences of the women on the course and the course outcomes. Whatever subject is covered and whatever methods are employed, it is important that opportunities are provided to build a supportive and caring group.

Assessment

There is an inherent tension here in that if courses place importance on the experiences of women, then how can this be assessed in a supportive way? It is therefore essential that where assessment is seen as an important part of the process, high priority is given to support and guidance through that process.

Progression

As argued earlier, women-only provision can be criticized if it leaves women in the same position at the end of the course as they were in at the beginning. For this reason the progression from the course needs to be considered and provision made for women to have individual advice and guidance about possible progression routes.

Recommendations and guidelines

At the outset of the study the aims were stated as:

- to analyse and appraise the curriculum design, course content and methods of teaching and learning on women-only courses;

- to identify the benefits and disadvantages of women-only provision;
- to provide guidelines for providers on the development of women-only courses.

The main body of the report (Coats *et al.* 1988) contains the analysis and appraisal of the content and methodology of women-only courses. Using this analysis, it is possible to classify the benefits and disadvantages of women-only provision.

Benefits: for individual women

Women-only provision:

- allows women to gain confidence from shared experiences and group support in a non-threatening environment;
- encourages women to locate their own personal experiences in a wider social context and thus understand those experiences;
- provides a secure base from which to go out into wider society and to which women can return for further support and encouragement.

Benefits: for society

Women-only provision:

- provides a transitional process for women returning to paid employment after a period of full-time domestic responsibility;
- encourages women to gain experience in 'non-traditional' activities before entering areas of work that are currently occupied mainly by men.

Disadvantages: for the women concerned

- The experience of women-only provision can only be transitional and women will lose the support of the group when they progress to further education, training or employment;
- The relevant practical support needed may not be available in other provision.

Disadvantages: for the providers

- Women-only provision is accorded low priority, limited resources and a marginalized position in most institutions and organizations;
- The image of women-only provision can arouse antagonism and sexist reactions based on fear and prejudice.

Recommendations

There is a sense in which all the recommendations relate to good practice in adult education generally. Nevertheless, apart from the first two, there is a distinct and clearly identifiable women-only dimension to what is being recommended.

1 Aims and objectives

There should be clear aims and objectives in terms of:

- target group
- content
- outcomes.

Tutors, students and anyone else involved in the provision needs to be aware of them.

2 Continuity

There should be continuity between planning, recruitment and delivery. If there is unavoidable change in the personnel involved then care should be taken to ensure as full an understanding as possible of the assumptions behind, and implications of, the stages already gone through. There are consequences here for staff development (see Recommendation 12).

3 Response to need

The course should respond to the needs of women, rather than to economic, political or institutional needs. Women's role in the labour market varies with the changing demands of the economy and it is not enough merely to respond to those demands without giving due importance to the needs of the women involved. Similarly, providing women's courses may fulfil a need for an institution, for example, one faced with falling rolls in the age 16–19 population. Providers of women's courses must be aware of the tensions that exist between responding to changing external circumstances while, at the same time, ensuring that the needs of the women returners are kept to the forefront.

4 Publicity

The publicity material needs to appeal to women and to be clear about the way the course will enable them to return to either education or to work. This can be done by appropriate use of pictures, graphics and languages.

5 Initial enquiry

The response to the initial enquiry should be friendly and supportive of women, many of whom have memories of education associated with failure. A friendly and personal letter can make the difference between a woman deciding to pursue her enquiry or not. Reception staff and those who deal with telephone enquiries should be well informed about the likely concerns of returning women and be able to treat them sympathetically.

6 Interviewing

The interview process should be well thought out, carefully planned and skilfully conducted. Those involved in interviewing should be aware of the special needs of women returning to education and training. For example, they should be able to:

• discuss practical arrangements for child care and travel;
• build confidence on the part of the student;
• look at the expectations of the student in relation to what the course has to offer.

If a full interview is not required, a pre-course meeting should be held at which these issues can be raised and women can be helped to decide if the course is appropriate for them.

7 Handbook

There should be a comprehensive, easy to read and attractive course handbook. Sections on rationale, content, assessment etc. can be written in a way that is supportive of women returners, giving guidelines of what is expected of them and indicating ways in which course objectives can be achieved.

8 Tutors

Tutors are crucial to the whole process. Women tutors need to be appointed who are:

• skilled
• experienced, and
• sensitive to the needs of women.

They need also to be able to encourage the development of a group dynamic which is supportive of all members of the group. Wherever possible, we would recommend that there be pairs of tutors, as cotutors are more likely to be able to work through potential conflict in the group and support one another and the students. There are implications here for staff development.

9 Teaching and learning style

There needs to be a teaching and learning style which:

- emphasizes the importance of group processes;
- acknowledges the importance of experiential learning;
- draws on the personal experiences of the women in the group;
- uses those experiences to move towards an understanding of women's place within society;
- focuses on the need to build confidence;
- enables women of all abilities to move forward within a supportive group.

The overall climate of learning should be one of cooperation and support, allowing women to value themselves and their achievements. It is our belief that it is only within women-only provision that this sort of climate can be generated.

10 Role models

Wherever possible the importance of the tutors as role models should be emphasized. In all the case studies there were examples of the tutors acting as role models for the women. In some cases the tutors were themselves mature women returners, either in other institutions or from the course that the students were currently taking. In other cases they were of the same ethnic background as some of the women; frequently they had experienced some of the personal difficulties that the women were experiencing. For the students to be able to identify with the tutors in this way was a positive experience.

11 Course team meetings

Regular course team meetings should be built into the structure of the course. The form, composition and frequency of the meetings can vary but the cohesion generated by collaborative decision making amongst a group of women is a key feature of many of the case studies. Team meetings should enable:

- modifications as the course is in progress;
- staff to support one another;
- potential problems to be aired before they become real difficulties.

The crucial factor, however, is the process by which issues are discussed. If students are also invited to attend, the students are given a sense of involvement which can itself contribute to their growing sense of confidence.

12 Staff development

The importance of staff development time and of paying part-time staff for attendance at staff development events and at course team meetings needs to be recognized. Adequate funding needs to be provided and staff development appropriate to women-only courses given, i.e. with an emphasis on the kinds of teaching and learning styles outlined in Recommendation 9. Staff development for reception and telephone staff also needs to be provided, in line with Recommendation 5.

13 Support systems

There should be good support systems for the students. For women returners these need to be of three kinds:

1. Practical support, such as with child care, travel, training grants etc.
2. Tutorial support, both individually and in groups. This needs to be tied into guidance and counselling, involving a special awareness of the vulnerability of many women returning to education and training after several years away from work. In addition to course sessions, individual tutorials can be offered to all the women on the course.
3. The possibility of access to professional counselling, if that is what is needed.

Overall, the support available needs to recognize the particular needs of women returners.

14 Base room

There should be a base room. There is evidence from all of the case studies that returning to learning can be stressful to women who have been at home for some time. For many a major difficulty are the physical surroundings in a large educational establishment and their return is eased by having a place of their own. For some it is essential that they have somewhere to take their children, as often play groups and crèches do not accept responsibility during the lunch hour.

15 Residential activities

Having a residential element to the course is something we would recommend wherever possible. It is especially important for women-only groups, giving both the opportunity for a 'breathing space' when the women are free from domestic responsibilities, and a future opportunity to develop good group relationships. For those who have never been away from home before without their families, it is also very important in developing confidence. For women a weekend away can be a valuable experience.

16 Work/community placements

Placements were an important part of a number of courses and were valued highly by the students. Their value is seen in terms of confidence building and in enabling the women to return to work in a more positive way. They are an aspect of women-only courses which enable the progression into work to be made more easily. For some, the transition into a mixed work environment is seen as threatening, and the work/community placement allows the transition to be made more gently and with the support of the group if needed. This is particularly important for women who are likely to go straight into work, rather than into further education or training. Where it is feasible to build in a work or community placement, we would recommend it.

17 Progression

Careful thought needs to be given to the question of progression. For progression to work well there has to be an understanding from the beginning about the aims and objectives of the course (see Recommendation 1). It is, however, important to recognize that individual women make decisions about the future in the light of their own circumstances and these have to be respected. If progression involves moving on to a mixed course, then the women-only provision should prepare women for those changes and support the women through them.

18 Validation

It is important for some women that there is validation at the end of the course. Validation may allow them to move through to higher education or may allow them to obtain work. However, validation is a problematic area and there are arguments both for and against it. On the one hand, there is the view that validation is counter to the ethos of women's courses, concentrating as they do on shared and cooperative learning. On the other hand, there is the argument that the acquisition of qualifications is important in moving women towards higher education or employment, and thus in giving them confidence.

If the validation process is flexible in terms of level and number of credits, then women can get something for what they do. What we would say, however, is that if there is to be validation then:

- it needs to be fully debated;
- it needs to be carried out in a systematic way;

- there needs to be good support and guidance systems which enable women returning to study to face the possibility of assessment in a non-threatening way.

19 Evaluation

The provision needs to be evaluated to see the extent to which the aims and objectives have been achieved. The evaluation techniques need to be flexible enough to accommodate a range of outcomes – as mentioned in Recommendation 17, the decisions of the individual women about how they 'use' the course have to be respected. We therefore recommend that a range of evaluation criteria be used, including, for example, attendance records as well as progression. Planned feedback and evaluation processes are important.

In addition to the recommendations and guidelines, the research process allowed us to develop an analytical tool for examining the curriculum of educational provision. Again, although this draws on women's education, it is appropriate for much wider use. This Framework for the analysis of the curriculum can be found in Appendix 2. It can be used as a checklist in designing or evaluating provision; as a challenge for those facing change and wishing to know if their existing provision is appropriate for women. While not all the components will apply to any given institution, the relevant sections can be used. It has also been used as a staff development tool for discussion and reflection.

9 | Education or Training? – the Significance of Women-only Provision

So far in this book I have used 'women's education' as a generic term that refers to all women-only provision whether it is officially recognized as education or training. In this chapter, however, I intend to look specifically at what might more accurately be called 'women-only training'.

Legally, the rules governing 'single gender' groups apply more to training than to education. Apart from provision designed to encourage and assist women returning to paid employment after a period of full-time domestic responsibility, the main thrust of the relevant section of the Sex Discrimination Act (SDA) is to encourage women (or men) to enter training for areas of employment in which they are regionally or nationally underrepresented. Thus women-only provision is essentially about training in preparation for a return to paid work. In practice, the distinction between education and training is unclear and further complicated by the division between vocational and non-vocational education. For women returning to education or training the difference may seem unimportant but for funding agencies, especially since the implementation of the Further and Higher Education Act (FHE) (1992), the distinction is critical (Powell 1992). The potential effects of the Act will be explored in the next chapter but it is useful to start with an overview of the main providers of, and funding for, women-only training.

Government-funded training in the UK is directed from the Department of Employment through the local Training and Enterprise Councils (TECs). They are responsible for funding local provision, some of which is targeted for women. The main providers, however, remain the further education (FE) colleges, through a whole range of vocational provision. In the past, many FE colleges ran women-only courses, both vocational and non-vocational, in non-traditional areas, in updating for women returners and in reorientation provision. Some institutions of higher education have provided courses for women – in both non-traditional areas of work and reorientation.

Funding for training has come from TECs, from LEAs, and from the European Community through the European Social Fund (ESF). ESF funding has been channelled through FE colleges and through the special women's training schemes with matched funding from the local authority. There has been some employer-funded training available for women, usually for women in paid work, except for some sponsorship schemes with FE colleges and other trainers. Finally, there are a number of private trainers who specialize in work with women, some of whom are extremely experienced and who provide high quality training. Most are very expensive. Individual women who can afford it have found their courses helpful but unless sponsored by an employer or through a TEC initiative, private training can only be appropriate for a small minority of women. The overall picture is patchy; the overall provision is inadequate, except in those skill areas that have always been stereotypically feminine.

There are several reasons why it is important to focus on women's training issues:

- Although there has always been a difference between vocational and non-vocational education, new legislation (the FHE Act) refines that difference and makes changes in funding which will have serious implications for provision and for fees and costs.
- Funding from European sources (through EC initiatives) has, in the past, been very important for women-only provision and continues to be so through the current New Opportunities for Women (NOW) initiative. This funding, and the regulations that govern its distribution, are for training, not education.
- Most of the workforce in the UK are undertrained in comparison to other members of the EC; women are even more undertrained than men.
- Opportunities for initial training and on the job training are far fewer for women than for men.
- Government training schemes, particularly for those who are unemployed, have offered some provision for women only. Changes in the management, provision and availability of these schemes have already reduced provision for women.

In all sectors of work in the UK women are less well-trained than men (McGivney 1992). There are several reasons for this. At the end of initial schooling, clear gendered patterns emerge. The same pattern is apparent in examination results and in the choice of subjects for FE or HE. Young women predominate in arts subjects, languages and biological sciences; young men predominate in maths and physical sciences, in computing and technology. It is not surprising that the same patterns are evident in all training and employment.

Initial training

Following the pattern of subject choices at school, women tend to train for occupations which are stereotypically 'feminine', mainly in the service sector. These jobs are generally less well paid and are of lower status than men's occupations.

All the evidence shows that there has not been any marked change in the kind of training taken up by young women and young men. In theory, all options are available to both; in practice, the training offered is to distinct gendered groups (see Table 9.1a and b). Women predominate in FE but cluster in educational courses and in those which lead to qualifications in clerical, catering, caring and other service industries. Young men are more likely to go on to Business and Technical Education Council (BTEC) and City and Guilds (C & G) courses or apprenticeships in a wide range of subjects (see Table 9.2).

In-service training

While in employment, women are offered fewer training opportunities than men and those that are available are at a lower level. More men than women participate in training opportunities during work. Initially, women may be trained to perform specific tasks and may receive in-service training to perform new tasks or operate new equipment, but they are less likely to be selected for further training or for advancement. Employers are generally more reluctant to invest in the training of women employees in case they decide to give up work for family reasons and the training investment is wasted. The optimum age for promotion and training to upgrade skills is for people in their late 20s and 30s. These are the years when women are most likely to be out of the workforce if they take a career break. Women who return to work after raising a family are thought not to be interested in advancement and therefore are not offered training opportunities. Some may have lost the confidence to put themselves forward for promotion.

Out-of-work training provision

For women who are not currently in paid employment, opportunities for training are restricted. Most unwaged women do not qualify for benefits, do not register, and therefore are not classified, as unemployed. The criteria that make training provision available for the unwaged and unemployed are continually changing. However, it is training provision for the unwaged that is attractive to many women and which may offer women-only alternatives.

Therefore, in most training opportunities – for school leavers before employment; in on-the-job training; in schemes for the unemployed or for those returning to the labour market – the same gendered patterns exist, with a few notable exceptions. The pattern shows no sign of changing apart from a small increase for women in managerial categories (McGivney 1992).

The inadequacy of training provision for women has been highlighted in two major national publications. In a discussion paper published by the Equal Opportunities Commission (EOC 1990) it was reported that the main training demands for women are for:

Table 9.1a Numbers and percentages of female home students continuing their education aged 16 and over, by age and type of course, 1989–90

	Age at 31 August 1989							All students
	16	17	18	Total 16–18	19–20	21–24	25 and over	
Numbers (000s)								
Total population	373	400	429	1,202	864	1,837	.	.
Full-time and sandwich students								
Schools	147	98	12	258	2	–	–	259
Further education	81	69	35	185	16	10	28	239
Higher education	–	4	47	52	115	76	51	293
Universities	–	2	24	26	56	34	16	132
Undergraduates	–	2	24	26	56	26	9	117
Postgraduates	–	–	–	–	–	8	7	15
Polytechnics and other HE courses	–	2	23	26	59	42	35	161
Total full-time and sandwich students	229	172	94	494	133	86	78	792
Part-time students								
Further education	77	65	57	199	114	306	1,446	2,065
Day students	44	37	21	102	44	112	570	828
Adult education centres	4	1	3	9	22	81	315	428
Other	40	35	18	93	22	30	255	400
Evening only students	33	28	36	97	70	195	876	1,237
Adult education centres	19	11	14	44	36	134	520	735
Other	13	18	21	52	34	60	356	502
Higher education	–	–	3	3	10	27	125	166
Universities	–	–	1	3	1	3	20	23
Open University	–	–	–	–	–	2	40	42
Polytechnics and other HE courses	–	–	3	3	10	22	65	100
part-time day	–	–	2	2	8	16	47	73
part-time evening	–	–	–	–	2	6	18	27
Total part-time students	77	66	60	202	124	333	1,571	2,231
All full-time and part-time students	306	238	153	697	257	419	1,649	3,023

Source: DE (1991)

Table 9.1b Numbers and percentages of male home students continuing their education aged 16 and over, by age and type of course, 1989–90

	Age at 31 August 1989							
	16	17	18	Total 16–18	19–20	21–24	25 and over	All students
Numbers (000s)								
Total population	396	421	449	1,266	900	1,903	.	.
Full-time and sandwich students								
Schools	141	96	14	251	2	–	–	253
Further education	71	55	32	158	16	10	19	204
Higher education	–	4	49	54	127	95	47	323
Universities	–	2	29	31	70	47	17	166
Undergraduates	–	2	29	31	70	34	9	145
Postgraduates	–	–	–	–	–	13	8	21
Polytechnics and other HE courses	–	2	21	23	57	48	30	157
Total full-time and sandwich students	212	155	95	462	146	105	66	780
Part-time students								
Further education	94	97	81	272	102	172	600	1,146
Day students	74	81	61	216	57	60	190	524
Adult education centres	3	1	1	5	7	24	65	102
Other	71	80	60	211	50	36	125	422
Evening only students	20	16	20	56	45	112	410	623
Adult education centres	11	6	7	24	23	73	201	322
Other	8	11	13	32	22	39	209	301
Higher education	–	1	8	9	28	44	150	231
Universities	–	–	–	–	–	4	27	31
Open University	–	–	–	–	–	2	44	47
Polytechnics and other HE courses	–	1	7	8	27	39	79	153
part-time day	–	1	7	8	25	30	54	118
part-time evening	–	–	–	1	3	8	24	36
Total part-time students	94	98	89	281	130	216	750	1,377
All full-time and part-time students	307	253	184	743	276	321	816	2,157

Source: DE (1991)

Table 9.2 Students enrolled on further education courses leading to specified qualifications by age, sex and mode of attendance, Autumn 1989 (000s)

Age at 31 August 1989	BTEC[1] SCOTVEC[2]	Royal Society of Arts	City and Guilds	GCSE GCE CSE SCE	Other specified courses	All courses leading to specified qualifications				
						United Kingdom	England	Wales	Scotland	Northern Ireland
Students aged 16–18										
Full-time and sandwich										
Males	65.9	0.4	26.2	43.8	9.6	145.9	122.8	7.8	9.5	5.8
Females	59.9	8.5	25.5	53.5	30.4	177.8	151.5	10.0	9.3	7.1
All persons	125.9	8.9	51.7	97.3	40.0	323.7	274.3	17.7	18.8	12.9
Part-time day										
Males	64.7	1.3	124.0	8.5	7.6	206.1	166.3	8.6	23.7	7.6
Females	30.9	9.8	27.2	11.0	7.0	85.9	65.2	2.7	13.7	4.3
All persons	95.6	11.1	151.2	19.6	14.6	292.0	231.5	11.3	37.4	11.8
Evening only										
Males	3.3	0.6	7.5	23.1	4.6	39.1	34.0	1.1	2.9	1.2
Females	3.2	12.1	3.0	32.3	6.4	57.0	47.5	2.0	5.2	2.2
All persons	6.5	12.7	10.5	55.4	11.1	96.1	81.5	3.1	8.1	3.4
All modes										
Males	133.9	2.2	157.8	75.4	21.8	391.1	323.1	17.4	36.0	14.6
Females	94.0	30.4	55.6	96.9	43.8	320.7	264.2	14.7	28.2	13.6
All persons	227.9	32.6	213.4	172.3	65.6	711.8	587.3	32.1	64.3	28.2
Students aged 19 and over										
Full-time and sandwich										
Males	19.2	0.4	4.8	7.1	7.0	38.5	28.4	1.4	7.6	1.1
Females	17.3	3.3	6.1	7.9	10.4	45.0	33.0	1.9	8.6	1.6
All persons	36.5	3.7	10.9	15.0	17.5	83.5	61.3	3.3	16.2	2.7
Part-time day										
Males	44.1	2.9	67.4	15.4	19.6	149.4	122.9	6.2	16.8	3.5
Females	23.1	22.7	38.2	29.4	30.6	144.0	121.7	4.3	14.6	3.4
All persons	67.2	25.7	105.6	44.8	50.2	293.4	244.7	10.6	31.4	6.9

Evening only										
Males	17.2	8.8	51.5	58.2	31.1	166.7	142.8	5.5	14.5	3.9
Females	17.1	63.9	24.6	106.9	34.3	246.8	204.5	9.7	23.8	8.8
All persons	34.3	72.7	76.1	165.1	65.4	413.5	347.3	15.2	38.4	12.7
All modes										
Males	80.4	12.1	123.7	80.7	57.7	354.6	294.1	13.1	38.9	8.5
Females	57.5	89.9	68.9	144.2	75.4	435.9	359.2	15.9	47.0	13.8
All persons	137.9	102.0	192.6	224.9	133.0	790.5	653.3	29.0	85.9	22.3
Students all ages										
Full-time and sandwich										
Males	85.1	0.7	31.0	50.9	16.6	184.4	151.2	9.2	17.1	7.0
Females	77.2	11.8	31.6	61.4	40.8	222.8	184.5	11.8	17.8	8.7
All persons	162.3	12.6	62.6	112.3	57.4	407.2	335.6	21.0	34.9	15.7
Part-time day										
Males	108.7	4.2	191.5	23.9	27.1	355.5	289.2	14.8	40.4	11.0
Females	54.0	32.5	65.4	40.5	37.6	230.0	186.9	7.1	28.3	7.7
All persons	162.7	36.7	256.8	64.4	64.8	585.4	476.2	21.9	68.7	18.7
Evening only										
Males	20.5	9.4	59.0	81.2	35.7	205.8	176.8	6.6	17.4	5.1
Females	20.3	76.0	27.5	139.3	40.7	303.8	252.0	11.7	29.1	11.0
All persons	40.8	85.4	86.5	220.5	76.4	509.6	428.8	18.3	46.5	16.1
All modes										
Males	214.3	14.3	281.5	156.1	79.5	745.7	617.2	30.5	74.9	23.1
Females	151.5	120.3	124.5	241.1	119.2	756.6	623.4	30.6	75.2	27.3
All persons	365.8	134.6	406.0	397.2	198.6	1,502.3	1,240.6	61.1	150.1	50.4
All modes 1988										
Males	197.0	14.1	264.7	163.2	75.5	714.5	594.5	29.3	69.9	25.8
Females	136.6	114.1	119.7	242.5	109.2	722.2	595.4	29.2	72.4	27.7
All persons	333.6	128.3	384.3	405.7	184.7	1,436.6	1,189.9	58.6	142.3	53.5

Table 9·2 (Cont'd)

Age at 31 August 1989	BTEC[1] SCOTVEC[2]	Royal Society of Arts	City and Guilds	GCSE GCE CSE SCE	Other specified courses	All courses leading to specified qualifications				
						United Kingdom	England	Wales	Scotland	Northern Ireland
All modes 1985										
Males	181.0	7.7	232.2	157.4	56.6	634.9	521.5	25.5	70.7	17.2
Females	107.2	82.3	93.2	223.0	83.1	588.8	479.1	22.6	66.4	20.7
All persons	288.2	90.0	325.4	380.3	139.7	1,223.7	1,000.6	48.0	137.1	37.9
All modes 1979										
Males	156.7	..	341.1	130.4	61.2	689.5	570.9	30.9	68.0	19.7
Females	57.0	..	72.8	171.5	85.1	385.5	307.3	16.6	45.5	17.2
All persons	213.7	..	413.9	301.9	146.3	1,076.0	878.2	47.4	113.5	36.9
All modes 1975										
Males	73.9	..	419.0	163.3	69.7	725.9	621.2		87.4	17.3
Females	25.1	..	69.9	195.1	89.1	379.2	293.7		70.6	14.9
All persons	99.0	..	488.8	358.5	158.8	1,105.2	914.9		158.1	32.2

1 Including BTEC first and national certificates and diplomas.
2 SCOTVEC has superseded Royal Society of Arts and City and Guilds examinations in Scotland.
Source: DE (1991)

- the updating of existing skills
- the building of confidence and other general skills to assist the return after a career break
- training in new technology
- training to enable a change of occupation.

These are all areas where women-only provision is available, although demand outstrips supply.

A study carried out by the Women's National Commission (WNC 1991) on women returners made the following recommendations about training:

- The government should devise a nationally coordinated policy for training women returners. The training should be relevant, high quality and accessible.
- The government training establishments and career advisers should ensure that women returners have access to clear, readily available information on career and training opportunities, supported by proper counselling.
- The TECs should make provision in their programmes for women returners to update and extend their skills.
- The government should consider funding full-time and part-time training courses for women who have spent time at home caring for dependants.

These are all components that good women-only education and training has developed and provided in a variety of contexts.

Training for unwaged women

In the 1980s there was a marked increase in the options available to unwaged women who wanted to return to employment. Although the early TOPS courses were mainly in skills that were stereotypically feminine, women were able to update, improve or acquire new skills in a women-only environment, whilst receiving a small allowance and expenses. Early in the 1980s the original WOW courses were funded by the (then) MSC. Although not offering the in-depth experience of the longer educational NOW courses, WOW did provide a valuable opportunity for less qualified women and for those who needed to return to employment fairly urgently.

The main weakness of MSC-funded provision was that it did not recognize the need for funding child care, arguing that women who seriously intended to return to employment would have already made provision for any dependent children. They seemed unable to understand that women who were in training schemes would be unable to afford the cost of child care or make satisfactory arrangements until they earned a regular wage.

Changing from the Manpower Services Commission (MSC) to the Training Agency (TA) and from Wider Opportunities schemes to Employment Training programmes threatened provision for women and moved towards a more individualized solution to unemployment. Subsequently moving the responsibility for training from centralized control to regionalized Training and Enterprise Councils (TECs) has resulted in a more localized service that actively involves and considers the needs of local employers. While some of the arguments for localized training provision are sound – training in response to local needs means that jobs should be available and skill shortages met – it has meant that provision for certain groups is dependent on local initiatives. Although there have been national directives to TECs and agreed priority categories, the training for women that is available in any given locality depends not just on local need but on the awareness and commitment of individual TEC officers.

Payne (1991), in a study of women who had taken the old government-funded TOPS courses, shows how successful they were in contrast to the individualized, employer-led training now available. She argues that women – particularly women returners – will be disadvantaged if training provision is market led and locally determined.

> The Government policy that the costs of adult training must be borne primarily by employers and individuals without public subsidy will almost inevitably reduce opportunities for women. However irrationally, employers still tend to regard women employees as a risk, and do not provide as much training for them as they do for men. Training for women returners, who have yet to prove their commitment to the labour market, is viewed as even more of a gamble.
>
> (Payne 1991)

Even though many TECs are recognizing the needs of women, the length and breadth of provision is far less than that funded by the old MSC or TA. Where schemes do receive TEC funding, it is seen as 'pump priming' or exploratory, on the assumption that employers take over the responsibility for training once the need has been identified. However, the Women Returners' Network has been working closely with TECs and has launched a 'Programme for Partnership' with them. In their 1992 Directory (WRN 1992), they report that 16 TECs have joined. They also list the activities of the 82 TECs, 68 of whom report some initiative for women returners.

These initiatives include:

- resourcing centres and groups to support women
- courses for women returners
- recognizing the need and making provision for child care
- setting up networks and hotlines to support women returners
- providing guidance and advice services
- producing packs and publications for women and for employers
- encouraging open learning provision
- helping with enterprise initiatives
- responding to the needs of black women
- making provision for rural women.

Women and training – a wider perspective

There are many reasons why the stereotypical pattern in employment continues and is reinforced in training provision. For women returning to training
and employment it may well seem sensible to improve or update existing
skills rather than try to enter a completely new field, even though many of
the women's training schemes (WTS) have shown that women can enter and
do well in non-traditional areas of work. Changing stereotypical patterns is
not the only aim of women-only training provision, however.

The role of women-only provision in training is both training for work in
which women are regionally or nationally underrepresented and training to
address the needs of domestic returners. Good training schemes for women
combine both of these requirements.

One of the problems with training women to enter areas of work that have
traditionally been dominated by men is that women have to acquire the basic
skills before they are able to progress further, and need confidence raising
and survival skills that will enable them to compete in a male dominated
trade. During the 1980s a number of WTS were started. This is one of the
areas of women-only provision where funding from the ESF has been available,
although the procedures for obtaining funding are complex and have to be
matched by local authority support. These schemes were designed to provide
training in skill areas that had always been dominated by men, the so-called
'non-traditional' areas. These include manual trades like plumbing, carpentry
and joinery, painting and decorating, motor mechanics, computing and electronics and work in audio-visual areas.

Most schemes target women who have few or no qualifications and, in
addition to skills work, women attending receive help with study skills, personal
development, deciding on future options and job search. Although the skill
level attained in the initial course may be fairly basic, many women go on to
local colleges to gain further qualifications in their skill area; others go on to
employment or self-employment. Most use their new skills to benefit family
and friends.

It is possible to be critical of the limitations of non-traditional training for
women but the well established and well run schemes continue to provide a
valuable new experience and the possibility of further training or employment. Most of the schemes target women who have no or few qualifications,
working-class and black women, thus offering training opportunities to groups
who are often ignored by other training providers.

Other women-only training courses for those who want to re-enter the
workforce are those which offer updating of skills gained from previous training or work experience, such as courses in word processing and electronic
office procedures for women who previously had keyboard skills as typists.
Professional updating courses for women offer a similar experience for those
who previously worked in professions like teaching or nursing, accounting or
law and need to update their knowledge before returning to employment in

those fields. Funding for some updating provision has come from Europe (especially under the new NOW initiative) and from local TECs. The WRN has been supporting institutions and organizations seeking funding from Europe for this purpose.

There are however, several major problems in funding women-only training from either Europe or TECs:

- the total number of women who can benefit is always going to be small compared to the potential demand;
- such provision is unevenly distributed geographically and many women live too far from appropriate training opportunities and may not be mobile;
- no overall strategy for women's training exists; it is piecemeal and uncoordinated;
- no secure funding is available – funding is short-term and has to be applied for annually;
- training is only provided in certain skills and trades and some of these trades are ones which have been particularly hit by recession;
- the criteria for funding changes frequently.

The new EC-funded 'New Opportunities for Women' (NOW – but not to be confused with courses of that title) is part of the Third Medium-Term Action Programme on Equal Opportunities for Women and Men (1991–5) (Commission of European Communities 1992). This initiative, which has been allocated 300 million ECU, is a good example of how funding from Europe demonstrates a real tension in providing training for women. On the one hand, it is to be welcomed as an initiative which recognizes the need for an extension in women's training and employment opportunities and demonstrates many of the characteristics that have been argued as essential for good women-only provision. NOW encourages transnational partnerships and the sharing of good practice:

NOW's efforts are focused on three areas: new business creation, re-entry into working life and child care facilities.

NOW encourages measures to provide information, training and financial backing to women wanting to start up their own businesses. The early days of a fledgling business are often hard. It is a time when information and advice are most invaluable. This assistance will be continued during the early stages of development, when women are in search of financial backing and training appropriate to the needs of their businesses.

Training schemes to help women re-enter the labour market will also be developed with reference to the particular needs of specific groups of women: long-term unemployed women often need career guidance and new qualifications to re-enter working life; women wishing to return to work after having raised a family must be able to take stock of their skills and regain their self-confidence before embarking on training and mapping out a career plan.

NOW pays particular attention to child care facilities. Adequate and appropriate facilities are essential, indeed, if work obligations are to be reconciled with family responsibilities. NOW acts in two ways here: by financing crèches and day nurseries in Objective One regions and by subsidizing the cost of child care for women in vocational training.

(CEC January 1992)

By March 1992, 32 projects had been successful in obtaining funding from NOW. A later edition of the newsletter reports:

Successful projects [in the UK] were chosen by a committee of experts which has been specifically set up for NOW. Those experts represent key training providers within Great Britain and will form the support structure for NOW. This novel approach to the co-ordination of NOW will ensure that valuable expertise gained through this new initiative will be widely disseminated.

Priority was given to projects which included child care provision and which looked at the validation and certification of training, including the accreditation of prior learning. The wide range of projects addresses all levels of qualifications from improving existing skills to higher level skills. These elements will provide the framework for the transfer of expertise within the Community and guarantee the success of the NOW initiative.

(CEC March 1992)

On the surface this seems like a good initiative from which to obtain funding for women-only provision, but there are problems. Earlier initiatives had encouraged individual schemes and colleges to apply for ESF funding. While this was a complex and time consuming task, it made the application process open to all. In fact, some local authorities and networks combined their expertise and supported the applications of their members. Now in the UK all applications are to be channelled through a 'committee of experts' before being allowed to approach the EC. Without wishing to question the expertise of the members of this committee, they are, in effect, gate-keeping; they are deciding who should apply. For example, in one of the early rounds several universities and polytechnics were successful in getting funding for 'professional updating' courses. While not wishing to deny the need for such courses, women who qualify for them are unlikely, by definition, to come from the most disadvantaged groups of women returners. By December 1992 there had been two rounds of applications processed; 41 applications were approved in the first round and 50 in the second. At this point the total funding available in Great Britain for the five-year NOW initiative had been fully committed.

Other training facilities do exist for those who have the resources to pay for them, but private training is rarely appropriate for women. Even where such training is of a high standard, it is expensive unless fees are paid by TECs or an employer. By definition women returners rarely qualify for employer-funded provision unless there is a very real shortage of labour in a particular field. For many women there is no option but to find – or to have help in finding – free training or a job that will utilize the skills they already have and provide some prospect of advancement. For other women all that is available are temporary or part-time jobs, offering low pay, low status and no possibility for further training.

Given that most women, whether they are in paid work or not, also have responsibility for all the domestic tasks and the care of children, it is not surprising that many prefer to study, train or work part-time. What is invidious is that those women are penalized in several ways.

Those in part-time education generally receive no grant; it has to be paid for, sometimes at full cost, unless the woman is dependent on benefit. Part-time training is rarely available except in basic skills. Part-time employment, usually temporary and insecure, is lower paid. Even in professions like teaching, the existence of supply and sessional work carries no employment rights, overtime, holiday or sickness pay. Part-time workers are rarely offered training opportunities unless they attend in their own (unpaid) time.

In response to the skills shortage and the so-called 'demographic trends' of the late 1980s, many colleges reduced their educational provision for women and offered more vocational training. In one survey of colleges in the eastern regions of England (Coats 1991), there was a noticeable decrease in reorientation and return to learn courses but an increase in courses designed to help women return to work. Whilst some of these had advice and guidance, confidence building and personal development components, others were simply skills updating in response to local employer needs. As mentioned earlier, while this may mean, in the short term, more actual jobs for women, it does reduce the options available to them.

Other developments in training provision for women

Two recent developments that have significance for women's training are the introduction of the scheme for National Vocational Qualifications (NVQs) and the increasing use of the Accreditation of Prior Learning (APL). The Further and Higher Education Act, funding from Europe and from the TECs all require that courses be accredited. In many cases these will be vocational qualifications in the form of an appropriate NVQ. This has implications for the content of the course and for the prescribed outcomes. Flexibility, negotiation and the ability to respond to the needs of the group may have to be sacrificed. Accreditation can be a rigid constraint.

However, any scheme that recognizes the achievements of both women and men, which records their attainments on training courses and credits skills developed through experience, has to be welcomed. Although it is possible to see these trends as a way of increasing the 'qualifications' of the work force without major investment, those involved in women-only provision for women returners have always argued that many of the skills used in the domestic arena are transferable to the world of paid work and should be recognized and rewarded.

In some APL schemes, women have been encouraged to provide evidence of their skills and competences gained in the domestic workplace and through voluntary and community involvement. The potential for women's skills to be recognized and accredited in this way is enormous, although most of the work has tended to focus on business administration. Exercises that allow women to regain confidence through realizing that their skills are transferable are often part of women-only provision. Many good courses for women returning to work have used a portfolio approach to identify and record their skills (Coats 1990). It seems that this recognition is long overdue, without the elaborate schemes for 'mapping' the skills of unpaid work that are currently underway. APL and NVQs are devices for accreditation that should be used if appropriate – tools for a purpose and not hoops through which women have to jump.

This chapter has focused on women-only training – its development and current changes. Changes in provision that are in response to changing circumstances in themselves should not be seen as threatening, if they retain the essential components of good practice. Some changes in women-only provision, however, appear to be threatening good practice and reducing its availability. In the final chapter, the nature of these changes and the reasons for them are explored more thoroughly – and a key question is raised. Can the current changes in education and training be perceived as part of a general 'backlash' against women?

10 | Women's Education – Challenging the Backlash

This book has attempted to document the development of women's education since the 1970s and to examine the distinctive characteristics that make such provision for women successful. This final chapter will draw together the arguments for women-only education in the light of changes in government policy and legislation on education and training, which threaten some of the existing structures and provision. In focusing on women's education, it is important to note also the implications for women who wish to progress to further and higher education.

It is important to stress that there have been some positive gains. Since the early 1970s there has been a marked increase in the types of education available for women, although the provision has been patchy and insufficient. Overall, much has been achieved, both by those who provided opportunities for only women and by those who make provision for women to participate in mixed groups. Although some providers have reservations about the need for women-only provision, there is generally a recognition of women's need for education and training and the term 'women returners' has become widely used.

There is a greater awareness of the practical difficulties that women face when they re-enter education or training – the most notable being provision for children. Not all institutions accept that 'mothers' have a right to education, but many provide or are seeking to provide some form of crèche or nursery. Although totally inadequate for the numbers concerned and in many cases too expensive for students to use, all institutions of higher education and many further education colleges now have some child care provision. The need to timetable courses within the school day and during the school term is recognized, though not always accommodated.

Other positive changes can be detected. All over Great Britain, in institutions, organizations and schemes, there are examples of good practice in women-only provision. There are various publications which describe case studies, document good practice and include guidelines for providers (Replan 1991a, b, c). There are many hundreds of individual women and teams of tutors who have considerable expertise in responding to the needs of women; some have produced and shared materials and lists of resources.

Although there is no single organization which coordinates this expertise and these resources, there are networks and groups committed to increasing and improving educational opportunities for women. Provision for unwaged women was greatly enhanced and encouraged during the 1980s by the DES-funded Replan programme. Projects, publications, conferences and groups all contributed to give women's education a higher profile nationally. Many providers benefited from support offered by that programme.

Since its inception the Women Returners' Network has been active in doing research, holding conferences, producing publications, encouraging networks and making sure that the needs of women returners are kept on the agenda. Even a cursory look at the latest WRN Directory gives some idea of the range and number of courses available to women.

A comparison between the original directory (produced in 1987) and that produced five years later (WRN 1992) gives some indication of the trends in women's education and the changes that have occurred. Although the directory cannot claim to be exhaustive, this annual volume does provide the most comprehensive national survey of what is available for women at any given time, including both women-only provision and mixed provision that is particularly appropriate for women.

Over the past five years, several trends emerge:

- a marked decrease in general reorientation provision but an increase in courses encouraging women to return to work;
- a marked decrease in women's studies provision, especially of short courses not leading to a qualification;
- a considerable increase in vocational courses, particularly those which update skills or knowledge;
- a huge increase in the number of 'access' courses, leading to entry to higher education. (These can only be designated as women-only when they provide access to a non-traditional area, for example, Access for Women into Engineering.)

The swing away from the more general reorientation or 'return to learn' courses to a more vocational 'return to work' emphasis has to be seen in the light of other changes to the structure and funding of education and training provision generally.

As Chapter 9 indicated, currently we are experiencing a time of major change in both education and training structures and funding – changes which can potentially threaten the existence of women-only provision. These changes are explored more fully later in the chapter. The need for major changes is often explained in terms of economic necessity which conceals the damage that is being done.

In the late 1980s much emphasis was placed on demographic trends and in particular the significance of the decline of the birth-rate in the early 1970s, which led in the 1990s to a decrease in the numbers of young people aged between 16 and 19. A decline in the number of school leavers has implications for both further and higher education, as well as for the labour market.

In all sectors, it was suggested that women could be recruited to fill the shortfall, providing a 'window of opportunity' for women returners to re-enter education, training or employment. Indeed there has been an expansion in the number of women with dependent children who return to work after maternity leave, while their children are of preschool age and while their children are still at school (see Table 10.1). There has also been an increase in the number of women taking courses in FE and HE – both in women-only courses and on all provision for adults. (Actual figures are hard to obtain because there is always a delay in the availability of statistics and because those statistics that are available do not always take account of age or gender.)

For a brief period 'women returners' became a popular slogan and a topic for conferences, radio programmes, magazine articles and reports. However, the 'bandwagon' effect tended to obscure some very important details in the data. Clearly there was a decline in the birth rate and thus a reduction in the numbers of 16–19 year olds for a period of time (see Figure 10.1), but the rate of decline was class specific. The greatest decrease was in the number of young people from 'working-class' families – more accurately those in Social Class III to VI (Smithers and Robinson 1989). The decline was less significant for young people from 'middle-class' homes (see Figure 10.2).

In higher education, students from 'middle-class' homes have always been overrepresented. Therefore the demand for higher education places did not decline as some predicted and, with some exceptions, departments were not looking to top up their student numbers with mature students or women re-entrants. At the same time, it must be noted that the massive increase in 'access' provision did mean that more mature students applied for and entered HE, including many women (see Figure 10.3), but the 'window' to higher education was never wide open.

Where there was a shortage of school leavers was in specific skill courses in FE colleges and subsequently in specific skill areas of the labour market. These were areas where few women – especially mature women – had qualifications. The other openings for women were in low paid jobs normally filled by young people with minimal qualifications – in service industries, especially retail, and other unskilled areas. For these jobs, further educational qualifications or updating were not necessary and firms developed 'packages' to attract the woman returner. These included working term time only, with shortened hours to fit the school day. To fill the rest of the time, they employed students. Whilst at one level this seems a progressive move to recognize the dual responsibilities of women with families, the work itself was low paid, part-time, temporary and with no decent conditions of service. When the demographic trends indicated the availability for the labour market of more young people, women returners were discarded. The 'window' of opportunity was already closing.

The overall significance of the demographic trend was further modified by other events. The deepening of the economic recession meant that fewer jobs were available anyway, as more and more firms made redundancies in their permanent workforce. Redundancies were particularly high in the public

Table 10.1 Economic activity of women aged 16–59 with dependent children, 1973 to 1990: Percentages working full-time, working part-time, and unemployed by number of dependent children in Great Britain

Number of dependent children and economic activity	1973	1975	1979	1981	1983	1985	1987	1988	1989	1990
1 dependent child										
Working full-time	21	21	20	20	19	21	25	24	24	27
Working part-time	29	33	33	33	33	33	34	33	35	35
All working	50	54	53 }55	53 }58	52 }57	54 }59	59 }65	57 }62	59 }64	62 }66
Unemployed	..	..	2	5	5	5	6	5	4	4
Base = 100%	1638	1749	1638	1680	1361	1348	1382	1322	1272	1267
2 dependent children										
Working full-time	14	13	13	12	13	15	14	17	19	19
Working part-time	31	37	40	38	33	37	42	43	44	43
All working	46	50	54 }56	50 }54	46 }51	52 }56	56 }60	60 }63	63 }66	62 }65
Unemployed	..	..	2	4	5	4	5	3	3	3
Base = 100%	1726	1849	1692	1855	1437	1401	1382	1254	1336	1172
3 or more dependent children										
Working full-time	14	11	13	13	8	10	9	13	14	10
Working part-time	30	36	36	26	28	32	32	33	34	37
All working	44	48	49 }51	39 }44	36 }40	43 }46	41 }45	46 }49	49 }51	47 }50
Unemployed	..	..	2	4	4	3	4	2	2	3
Base = 100%	1091	1061	777	793	656	518	541	547	529	517
All with dependent children										
Working full-time	17	16	16	15	14	17	18	19	20	21
Working part-time	30	35	36	34	32	35	37	37	39	39
All working	47	51	52 }55	49 }54	46 }51	51 }56	54 }60	56 }60	59 }63	60 }63
Unemployed	..	..	2	4	5	4	5	4	4	3
Base = 100%	4455	4659	4107	4328	3454	3267	3305	3123	3137	2956

* Persons aged under 16, or aged 16–18 and in full-time education, in the family unit and living in the household.
Source: OPCS (1990)

Figure 10.1   18-year-old population in England and Wales

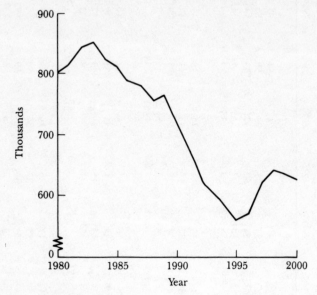

Source: Smithers and Robinson (1989)

Figure 10.2   18-year-old by social class

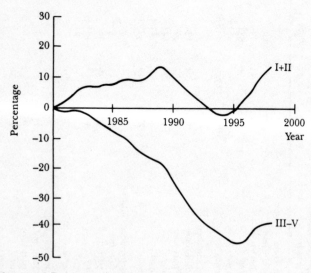

Source: Smithers and Robinson (1989)

Figure 10.3 First year mature home students[1]: by sex and establishment in Great Britain

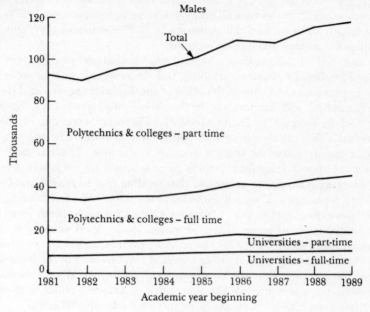

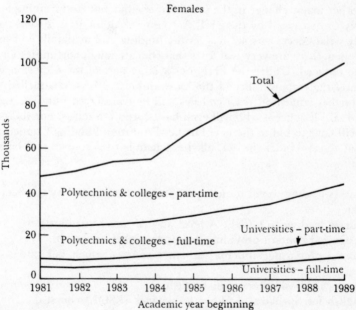

1 Excludes part-time students from the Open University
Source: OPCS (1992)

sector as local government services were reduced and community charge capping took effect. Women have traditionally been employed in the public sector, especially in clerical grades. Education departments, social services and public health authorities all employed large numbers of women. With the move to privatization and the reduction in the local tier of government, the openings for women have been reduced.

As outlined in the previous chapter, similar changes are apparent in the reduced funding for women's training and the reorganization of government training provision. With the disbanding of the Training Agency and dispersal of organization and funding to the localized, employer-led TECs, women have had to struggle to retain visibility. There are excellent examples of individual TECs collaborating with institutions and organizations to provide training opportunities for women but this is variable. There is evidence to suggest that now 'domestic returners' (i.e. women) are no longer a top priority category for training provision, that funding has decreased and facilities are being withdrawn. Coupled with this is the nature of TEC funding, much of which is exploratory or pump priming. Once a survey or needs analysis has been completed and some initial provision made, local employers are expected to take responsibility for the training needs that have been identified. That these needs are more those of the local employers than the local women means that any provision will be targeted and single exit. While this may lead to immediate employment in the short term, it may not equip women to be better qualified either vocationally or in wider educational terms.

Another major change in the provision of education and training for adults is likely to be caused by the FHE Act (1992). Although it is too soon to see exactly what effects this act has on the funding and availability of provision for women, there are very real fears that educational opportunities for women will be reduced. Under the FHE Act a large part of the provision which is currently the responsibility of the local authority (LA), channelled through their further education (FE) colleges will be transferred from the LA to the individual FE colleges who will each have corporate status. For their funding they will have to bid to the new Further Education Funding Council (FEFC) (Powell 1992). Under the act, all the 'schedule two' courses will be affected, including:

1. courses leading to vocational qualifications recognized by the Secretary of State,
2. courses leading to GCSE, A level and AS level qualifications,
3. recognized courses providing access to higher education,
4. courses preparing students for other courses which fall into categories 1–3,
5. courses for basic literacy in English,
6. English for Speakers of Other Languages (ESOL) courses,
7. courses to teach basic principles in mathematics,
8. in Wales, courses for proficiency or literacy in Welsh,
9. courses designed to teach independent living and communication skills to those having learning difficulties.

The remaining provision of FE colleges and of most adult and continuing education will be funded by LAs, but as part of their general budget. Even before the start of the first year of funding, the bids for adult education exceed supply. It is expected that most of that provision will be offered at full-cost fees, unless the LA has a firm policy designed to allow concessions to certain groups.

This will mean that most women will be denied access to courses unless they have the financial resources to pay for them. That the vast majority of unwaged women have no financial resources of their own means that unless providers find some way of supplementing concessionary fees, some provision, particularly for women only, may disappear. This threatens to close a very important progression route for women to access courses and to higher education. Many women do not have the confidence or circumstances to embark directly on a long access course or proceed directly into higher education. They need time to reorientate, to discover their potential, to be supported through the process of change. Women-only provision which is not 'academic' or 'vocational' has provided the opportunity to prepare for future courses and to open up progression for many women. This is the provision which may be removed.

The most potentially damaging effect for women-only provision is the enhanced distinction between vocational and non-vocational courses. Under the new act, this distinction, which has always posed a problem for providers, will become enhanced. The most likely casualties are the reorientation courses – those like NOW and WOW which do not provide specific training in any one discrete area but which have been shown to be a vital type of provision for many women returning to education, training or employment.

Although the changes suggest that the funding of provision will be complex, the funding available for individual students may be even more complicated. Already there is confusion about which students qualify for reduced or concessionary fees, especially when applied to dependent women. Women who themselves claim benefit, or who are dependent on a partner who claims, usually qualify for concessions. Whether these concessions will continue is not known. Women who are unwaged and dependent on a partner who works are usually expected to pay their own fees. If courses are to be cost effective, the fees will rise. Many dependent women do not have access to finance of their own and their ability to pay may depend on their partner's approval.

Students at all levels will be affected by the move from grants – whether mandatory or discretionary – to loans. For various obvious reasons, loans to mature women students will be problematic. Mature students dependent on benefits face an even more complex decision. In some cases, they are financially better off on benefits with concessionary fees than on a grant or loan – but not always (Hyde 1992).

During the 1980s the availability of funding from the European Community has had a major impact on provision for women, particularly in funding courses and schemes which provide training in 'non-traditional' skills. European Community directives rarely address education. The differences in educational provision of individual member states have largely been ignored and adult education has had an even lower profile. Training provision, however, especially that which affects women, has been subjected to various directives and initiatives. Many of the current schemes initially received or continue to receive funding from the European Social Fund.

This changing funding raises two problems. Some providers for whom ESF funding ends have to find alternative sources; some have been successful in this, others have not. Changes in the criteria for funding and the introduction of new initiatives mean that providers have a complex task of reworking their applications to ensure new or continuing funding. Providers who were dependent on matched funding from local authorities may have to find other sources. The response to this by the Further Education Funding Council (FEFC) is not known. Some providers who received funding from their local authority have been assured of their commitment to supporting provision for women. Others will have to rely on support of their own colleges. The picture which emerges is very confused and many courses for women only are threatened. The most vulnerable are not the vocational courses or those which award a nationally recognized credit, but the original NOW type of reorientation provision which is not included under 'schedule two' of the FHE Act. Some of this provision may qualify as pre-access and thus be eligible for FEFC funding or for group counselling under EC funding but, for many providers of reorientation courses the future is bleak.

In a survey (Coats 1992b) of the funding of women-only provision which looked at both non-traditional and reorientation courses it was found that there was some cause for concern. Not only is some of the funding threatened, but, even more worrying, the nature of women-only provision is being challenged. Responses to a question asking if the 'women-only' nature of their provision was being challenged, respondents wrote such comments as:

- 'Women-only education and training is unnecessary';
- 'Integration is complete – it is no longer needed';
- 'Exclusive and expensive provision';
- 'Unnecessary/separatist/elitist/divisive';
- 'Expensive, especially crèches, low numbers';
- 'Men want "special" courses for them';
- 'Opportunities for unemployed men not addressed';
- 'Unemployed men need similar provision';
- 'If a male person approaches us, he would be just as welcome as the females';
- 'A man wanted to join the course – we enrolled him';
- 'Challenged on grounds of equal opportunities or equality of opportunity';
- 'Available spaces and increased unemployment means more men on courses';
- 'We let in men to avoid the challenge'.

When questioned about funding and the reasons why the security of the provision was threatened, respondents gave the following reasons:

- transfer of funding to colleges and FEFC;
- the college will make the decisions, not the LEA;

- funding moved from Employment and Training Department to Education Department, therefore lower grant and insecure future;
- delays in ESF application lost us the local authority funding;
- local authority cuts in many areas;
- no increase in funding despite inflation;
- changes in ESF criteria;
- partnership funding is hard to find – more emphasis on income generation;
- may have to shift from developmental work to accreditation (NVQs);
- lack of commitment to permanent contracts – short term/sessional;
- funding for limited period – not threatened but transitional;
- cost per unit can be a problem because of child care;
- shortage of crèche places;
- shortage of funding for crèche;
- ever increasing cost of child care;
- merger of university and polytechnic sectors may reduce funding for non-accredited courses, therefore may have to raise fees;
- reduction in budgets and FHE Act;
- purchaser/provider model used;
- no mainstream funding and no renewal of three year plan;
- providers using local business sponsorship hit by recession;
- ESF shared between more courses in the college;
- fewer resources for planning and training;
- pressure to incorporate NVQs is utilitarian;
- qualification at end of course needed;
- grant/loans/fees issues for women students;
- low level of political support for women's training.

However, there were also encouraging signs and some optimism in replies such as:

- 'ESF funding can be used for guidance and that fits our courses';
- 'We have the new NOW funding';
- 'We are fortunate enough to be in a City Challenge Task Force area';
- 'Have had some (small) grants from TECs – for research and publications';
- 'Local TEC realizes women are part of the work force';
- 'This city has a commitment to work for women';
- 'FEFC will support accredited ESF courses';
- 'It is supported by college management, departmental staff and funding bodies';
- 'New nursery at college has improved facilities';
- 'Provision expanding 50 per cent per year because of demand';
- 'Course valued because it recruits/gives access to other courses at the college';
- 'Present principal very supportive (but he is retiring before incorporation)';
- 'This area of work (women returners) is part of our strategic plan and should continue';
- 'Expanding in all areas where funds can be attracted to the college';
- 'Funding from Europe is generous'.

One college wrote: 'Our women-only provision has expanded due to our policy and commitment to the needs of women. It is a constant struggle but not one that we are prepared to give up.'

The changes that are becoming evident in women's education and training in the UK are also reflected in other parts of Europe, so while any European initiative to fund women-only provision has to be welcomed, there is also cause for concern. Oglesby (1990) summarized very clearly the major issues for women in Europe as:

- changing welfare policies in European countries and the implications for education in social and personal terms;
- the changing regulations on EC nationality and the implications these will have for ethnic and political groups in minority positions in the countries in which they are living;
- major changes in educational policies in many countries, with predominant emphasis on education for industrial and commercial ends, often at the expense of cultural and personal development;
- industrial restructuring – a growth of part-time work in western Europe; unemployment is expected to rise significantly;
- internationalization and competition throughout the whole of Europe, with the introduction of the single European market in 1992;
- new technologies and the implications these have for educational systems and support services;
- ecological awareness and its subsequent effects on social and industrial initiatives;
- East–West détente.

Oglesby covers the implications of these trends for finance, level, access and curriculum of education, against which the impact of the Third Action Programme (which includes NOW) must be seen. But the European Community itself is changing and has to operate within the context of an enlarged Europe which includes both central and eastern European countries. These former Eastern bloc countries face their own particular problems, including the specific problems of women. Thus she sums up,

> The inevitable conclusion from reviewing the position of women in Europe is that the integration of women into the labour market, the continuous rise in education and training levels among women and the availability of child care in many but not all EC member states are not enough to enable women to achieve equal access to decision-making positions in society. They are not sufficient to break through the nature of existing structures.
>
> (Oglesby 1991)

In the UK as well, this is a period of change in funding (the FHE Act), in educational provision (especially access), in training (TECs) and through the new initiatives in Europe.

This is also an era of change in ideology and in ideas. Since 1979 the

Conservative government has reflected the dominant ideology of individualism and the free market, but have been modified by more conservative views of women. This has been reflected in media-led stories of post-feminism and what has been called the 'backlash against women' (Faludi 1992). In the UK we have not seen examples of the 'backlash' as overt as those described in the United States by Faludi (1992), but there is a growing fear that some of the current changes in women's education and training could be part of a growing challenge to women's demands for equality.

Stories of the so-called 'post-feminist' era can be countered with statistics which show that despite the Women's Movement, the position of women has changed little over the past 20 years. Attitudes to the position of women have changed even less. Although the media (and many men) may claim that women now have 'equality', the evidence demonstrates that this is untrue. In fact, given the struggles since 1975 to implement equal opportunities for women, it is discouraging to see that in the labour force so little has changed.

What does give cause for concern is the attitude to, and action on, issues of 'equal opportunities'. In the 1980s there seemed to be a steady growth in equal opportunities policies and in codes of practice, though a slower growth in implementing action plans and the monitoring of progress. Evidence for this is hard to quantify but there seems to be a stalemate, if not steady erosion, in equal opportunities provision. The rhetoric is still in place with most authorities, institutions and organizations claiming to have an equal opportunities policy but very little evidence of changing practice. Having a policy is seen as sufficient – if only for legal protection and as a statement of intent – but there is, in many cases, very little intention of change. There are no resources for monitoring or for training, no long-term investment. With the education sector in a constant state of change, with too many other pressures on performance, equal opportunities gets put onto the back boiler – not discarded but not implemented. Is this evidence of backlash? Certainly it is the gender component of equal opportunities which has taken most of the attack as being no longer necessary. Some evidence of the misinterpretation of the meaning of equal opportunities can be seen in the responses to the survey quoted above.

Equal opportunities is about preventing discrimination and reducing disadvantage. The SDA sections covering women-only provision are to reduce the imbalance and the segregation of women in the workforce, to widen possible options for every woman. Provision for re-entry after domestic responsibilities is to reduce the effects of the 'career break', to counteract the effects of the interruption on women's progress and to enable women to attain their full potential. Single sex provision for women who have had full-time domestic responsibilities is not the same as provision for men who have been unemployed. This is not to deny that those who have been unemployed, both women and men, do not need specific education and training provision to meet their needs – the Replan programme showed how essential and how effective such provision could be. But women-only provision for unwaged women returners should never be expected to include unemployed men. Such provision is not sexist or separatist. It is designed for a specific and necessary purpose and cannot by definition contravene equal opportunity criteria.

Another challenge to women-only provision comes from the dominant ideology of individualism, which relies on market forces and self-interest. This approach is not likely to be sympathetic to the provision of a women-only group, based on principles of shared learning and mutual support (unless, of course, such a group can afford the full fees for a course). Alternative provision for women has to be watched with caution. The last few years have seen a considerable increase in books and 'open learning' packages for women returners such as those produced by the Domino Consultancy (1990), the National Extension College (Clark and Hardy 1991) and Springboard (Willis and Daisley 1990). While some of these packages contain excellent material, they are costly and, if completed in isolation, can be dangerous. Instead of enabling women to recognize their abilities and raise their confidence, their negative effects can compound women's feelings of inadequacy. All of these packages are best used in a group situation, with tutor support. However, the cost may be prohibitive unless subsidized by other funding.

The other cost-cutting trend which has to be challenged is the tendency to provide one day events for women returners. These can be excellent occasions for making women aware of what is available and for encouraging them to join women-only courses or proceed to other relevant training. However, thorough information, guidance and advice which is the hallmark of good provision for women is less effective when given in isolation or at a one-off event. For many women the process of reorientation takes much longer and needs the special support of the group and specialist tutors.

One of the major problems for women is that any extension of their involvement in the work force has not been accompanied by other changes in the domestic workplace, or in relationships with their partners (Kiernan 1992). Most women still carry the dual role of employment plus the responsibility for household tasks and child care. Many women, despite legislation for maternity leave, take far longer than the maximum allowed and, when they do return to paid work, do so on a part-time basis. While provision in the UK for paternity or parental leave is so inadequate (compared to most of the rest of Europe), many women will continue to take time out of employment. In periods of recession and unemployment they will be encouraged to do so. Indeed, the 'conservative' view of the position of women is a very strong component of the backlash. Every social disaster, from abortion to sterility to divorce and delinquency, has been blamed on women wanting equality and rejecting their 'natural' role. While most of the men in positions of power and in control of funding would deny this if challenged, their attitudes reflect an unrecognized assumption that women's place is in the home and not in education, training or employment. If economic constraints and cuts in funding mean that some provision has to be reduced, it is not surprising that women's education should be seen as disposable.

This same ideological argument has an effect on women too. On the one hand we suffer from the 'superwoman syndrome' and feel inadequate and guilty if we cannot cope with the double burden or fail to achieve; on the other hand, many of us feel inadequate or guilty because we are neglecting our homes and families in pursuit of what seems to be selfish personal satisfaction and growth.

If women are to be allowed to develop fully as individuals or to contribute effectively to society as a whole, some 'compensation' is needed on the grounds of equity or economic necessity. If women are *expected* to take time out of employment to bear and raise children, they should equally *expect* provision to help them return to work after that period.

Women's education demands that adequate and appropriate provision is available for those who need it and that women-only space be made available for those who choose it. Different entry points and different routes at different levels are needed to help women back into education or training. This means that expert admissions advice and guidance are also needed to help women choose the most appropriate option.

Above all, sufficient and secure funding is needed so that those women who have few or no resources are not prevented from taking part in the education or training options available. The three demands of the NIACE Women's Conference held in Brighton on International Women's Day 1992 are still relevant here (Coats and McGivney 1992):

- We need a coherent education and training policy which takes into account the different and varied circumstances of women.
- We need adequate funding for provision which does not discriminate between modes, levels and purpose.
- We need adequate understanding and provision for carers.

Women-only education is seen as both subversive and separatist only by those who fear its effects. If there is a backlash against women on either economic or equality grounds, it will be resisted and challenged. We have learned a lot in the past 20 years and we are not going to lose it now. In the book entitled *Grassroots Education for Women in Europe* (EBAE 1992), Birte Lykkegaard writes about a course for women called 'Think, wish, go ahead!' and concludes with the following quotation: 'To dare is to lose foothold for a little while. Not to dare is to lose oneself.'

This attitude applies to many of the individual women who have discovered themselves through educational experiences shared with other women and also to all the women tutors who have challenged organizations and institutions to provide education which is appropriate for women.

Appendix 1
Women-friendly Approaches to Teaching and Learning: an Overview of Selected Papers (from Pravda 1991)

The programme

- Timing, cost and place appropriate;
- Organization takes account of women's family commitments, conflicting demands from work, family, friends;
- Maximum accessibility;
- Provides/facilitates resources for care of dependants;
- Reaches out to women wherever they are;
- Recognizes the need for women tutors;
- Recognizes the needs of women tutors;
- Rewards women tutors for their skills and commitments;
- Congruence between content and process if classroom interaction reflects feminist principles;
- Integration of egalitarian content and process;
- Encourages women to push themselves towards academic and personal excellence;
- Incorporates field-based action;
- Connects ideas to liberating action;
- Bias towards practical training, often including work placement advice on appropriate qualifications and exit routes;
- Multi-exit courses;
- Support scheme:
  - easy access to learning resources
  - child care provision
  - easy access to advice and information
  - support from other women
  - responsiveness to needs of different groups of women
- Combination of independent study with scheduled on-site activities and study centres.

Course content

- Uses feminist analyses to examine lived experiences of women, including early socialization;
- Values women's contributions to knowledge production;
- Analyses differences between received and objective, personal and objective knowledge;
- Applies gender analyses to the production of 'malestream' knowledge;
- Values and uses subjective experience of women and special behaviours characteristic of women;
- No stereotyping in language, examples and images;
- Acknowledges domestic role;
- Respects individuality of women;
- Values attributes of women, uncovers 'female' qualities;
- Student controlled or negotiated curriculum;
- Student–teacher collaboration;
- Connections between course content and life transitions, transition-centred projects;
- A portrayal of women in traditional disciplines;
- Ways in which women are oppressed and alternatives for liberation;
- How personal oppression is tied to the political, economical and social structure of society;
- Gain knowledge to better control their lives;
- Fundamentally different notions of knowledge, its generating and validating: dialectic, interactively created and tested through experience; knowledge as an ever-evolving, mutually developing process;
- Incorporates central features of the Women's Movement into teaching;
- Self-definition instead of prevailing male definitions;
- Acquaint students with different feminist theories;
- Makes women a topic for study;
- Women's and men's experiences are equally valid sources for the construction of knowledge;
- Avoids overall generalizations which speak for us all; creates a more complex and composite picture or reality; generalizations are built inductively from specific individual experiences;
- Knowledge as a result of an inductive research process;
- New concept of personal growth; interdependence instead of dependence vs independence.

Teacher behaviour

- Encourages self-empowerment and transformative learning;
- Acknowledges differences in women's experiences as well as commonalities;
- Support of new feminists by established ones;

- Handles with sensitivity emotions caused by misogyny;
- Develops strategies for dealing with oppression;
- Ensures equal attention and respect for women and for men;
- Non-exclusionist language and imagery;
- Challenges only with support;
- Asks open rather than closed questions;
- Encourages all women to participate;
- Allows 'I do not understand';
- Encourages continuous and honest feedback;
- Teacher's emphasis on experiential learning will help empower older students;
- Facilitates learning rather than formal teaching;
- Avoids attitude of dominant ideology and universal and eternal truth;
- Makes legitimate perspectives of the world held by the oppressed;
- No imposition of a single right answer;
- Breaks the habit of looking to the teacher for the answers.

Design and production of materials

- Women are an integral part of the programme – do not 'add women and stir';
- Learning materials specifically for women;
- Avoid reinforcing gender stereotypes, particularly where materials will be encountered outside group situation;
- No patronizing by over-simplification and avoidance of technical terms;
- Should allow for variety of student activities;
- Interactive;
- Relate to practical context of use, drawing on student's experience.

Learning process

General

- Incorporate central features of Women's Movement into teaching, within the political context of feminism and Women's Movement;
- Anti-sexist teaching.

Deconstruction

- Deconstruct gendered experience of initial schooling;
- De-learn image of intellectual dependence;
- Endorse multiple options to accommodate women's heterogeneous and complex expressions of rage and objection to bias.

Acquaintance – solidarity

- Interpersonal activities to become acquainted;
- Structured as well as informal formats for getting to know classmates and break isolation;
- Festive procedures to build solidarity.

Cooperation

- Strengthen cooperative and collaborative processes instead of competitive and hierarchical ones: cooperative goal structuring, small discussion groups, cooperative projects as assignments (as methods of collaboration), group building, non-hierarchical ways of teaching, group learning environment;
- Shared learning environment – students and tutors both contribute;
- Democratic and egalitarian classroom process, anti-hierarchical teaching;
- Democratic group processes, list of function roles, rotation of leadership, democratized hierarchical views of leadership;
- Replace hierarchical authority with participatory decision-making: shared leadership, teacher, student, instructor and women experts from outside reciprocity;
- 'Connected' as opposed to 'separate' thinking/problem solving;
- Cooperative instead of disputative environment;
- Shared responsibility for peers' learning, community of learners, network, learning process mutually supportive;
- Transform isolated individuals into a cohesive group, building knowledge collectively, spirit of collaboration and shared knowledge, peer groups – from social grouping to formal learning partnerships.

Safety

- Build and maintain safe climate for giving voice, for questions and disclosures;
- Consciousness-raising, needs in confidence
- Produce an honest classroom atmosphere;
- I-messages give positive feedback;
- No exposure of any woman against her will.

Feelings

- Encourage to use feelings, intuition and imagination as resources/strengths for learning;
- Acknowledge affective as well as cognitive processes, integration of cognitive as well as affective learning;

- Acknowledge the role of emotions, attitudes and value assumptions in shaping our and others' view of the world – the subjective, personal element;
- Space to explore thoughts and feelings, acceptance of each others' responses, serious attention to differences between women, integrate and connect differing perspectives;
- Opportunity for creative expression.

Experience

- Relates all learning experience;
- Real life reflections and decisions;
- Allows experiential learning, reflectivity, connection of experience and emotions;
- Provide experience in solving problems and finding solutions collectively – they are partial and evolving;
- Connect experience with theory, theory with practice;
- Classroom activities and assignments derived from reward and generalize experience;
- Accentuate adult's strength as inductive learner.

Skills

- Student-centred teaching style;
- Self-directed learning intrinsic to feminist pedagogy;
- Confidence in skills etc. already possessed;
- Gain process skills;
- Focuses on perceived, not received, knowledge;
- Makes new ways of learning exciting and enjoyable;
- Flexible learning patterns to extend women's opportunities;
- Try unfamiliar roles in a supportive setting;
- Helps to identify and develop student's own learning skills;
- Devises strategies for continued learning.

Interaction – action

- Break the mindset of passivity and the unreflective taking of information;
- Activist notion of education as tool to gain and exercise power and organize social action – theory is related to action;
- Encourage interaction, experimental activities like theatre, role playing, movement, fantasy – interactive pedagogy.

Individualization – commonalities

- Explore and understand women's commonalities and differences;
- Help women give voice to their thoughts, dialogue;
- Encourage and value the contribution of each woman;
- Oral reports as public testimony.

Support – growth

- Support of women in personal change, personal and academic support groups, vehicle to cooperation, commitment to personal and social change;
- Counselling and other support mechanisms;
- Gain skills to better control their lives;
- Allows for progression by information and guidance;
- Prepares women for moving on by developing transitional skills;
- Work towards self-empowerment of individual women and the group, insights about conditions of women and reactions – 'gain power collectively' but ultimately exercise it individually.

Grading

- Grading – institutional requirements vs personal encouragement; identify own aims, student–teacher collaboration, contract grading.

Organization

- Workload and study period: consideration of women's multiple obligations and limitations in formalized learning experiences.

Appendix 2
Framework for an Analysis
of the Curriculum

Sections: 1 Values and ideologies
2 Course design and organization
3 Content and delivery
4 Evaluation and development

1 Values and ideologies

1a From where did the original idea come?
When was the course planned/designed/started?
By what process was the course conceived and planned?
What consultation was involved?
What outside bodies were involved?
To what extent was the course designed by the tutors? by others?

1b What are the stated aims of the course?
What are the aims as intended by the designers?
What are the aims as perceived by the tutors?
Do different tutors interpret the aims differently?
How well do the aims fit in with the aims of the institution/organization?
What institutional support is offered? (policy? management? resources?)
What (ideological/educational) values inform the design?

1c For what target group is the course designed?
Has research been done to determine the target group?
Has research been done to determine the need?
Does the target group change between courses?
What criteria for selection of students are used?
What are the minimum/maximum numbers accepted?

2 Course design and organization

2a Is the course free-standing or part of other provision?
What is the length of the course?
What days and hours?

Are tutorials programmed for individual students?
Is there a residential component to the course?

2b What are the sources of funding?
Is the funding secure from year to year?
Does the source of funding impose constraints on the course?
If so, what are these constraints?

2c What is the cost of the course to the students?
Do students receive payment or expenses?
Do students receive advice on their benefit/payment entitlement?
What form of child care is available?
What is the cost of child care for the students?
Who funds the child care?

2d How many tutors are involved?
For what hours?
Do tutors have other work with same institution?
Do tutors have other work with another institution?
Are tutors technically employed full or part-time?

2e What are the backgrounds of the tutors?
What subjects does each tutor cover?
What is the nature of the tutor group? (e.g. management; team teaching etc.)
Are tutor meetings timetabled into the course?
Do tutors have their own separate area?
Do tutors share responsibility for the course?
What opportunities exist for staff development?
What staff development has taken place?

2f How is the course publicized?
What course information/handouts/leaflets are available?
Where is information about the course available?
What profile is given to the 'women-only' description?
What is the application and registration process?
Is each student interviewed before starting the course?

2g Is the course located in a separate building?
Are the child care facilities in the same building?
Do students have to take responsibility for children in the lunch hour?
Do students have a safe area in which to leave their coats and belongings?
Do they have their own tea/coffee/lunch making facilities?
Do they have their own separate base room?

3 Content and delivery

3a What is the title of the course?
How is the course described?

What subjects are covered in the course?
What rationale underlies the choice of content?

3b How flexible is the content?
Can it be modified during the course?
Is it modified during the course?
Can it be modified between courses?
Is it modified between courses?
To what extent do students negotiate the content of the course?

3c What ideological framework is used?
Is the ideological framework identified?
Is theory included?
What is the balance between description and explanation?

3d What topics or themes are covered in the course?
What input materials are used?
Are the students' personal opinions/experiences used in content and delivery?
Are their opinions/experiences located in a wider context?
Is the emphasis on knowledge/skills/processes?

3e What teaching strategies are used?
Do they vary with different tutors?
Who decides on teaching strategies?
Can they be modified during the course?
Are they modified during a course?
Can they be modified between courses?
Are they modified between courses?

3f To what extent is group identity created?
How is the group identity created?
Are group methods/tasks used?
What is the size of groups/subgroups?
How are group members allocated?
Why is group identity considered important?

3g What is the tutor input/student output equation?
What type of input is made?
To what extent are verbal/written/visual inputs used?
What is produced by individuals/groups?
What kind of tasks are set?
Are right or wrong answers expected?
How are right and wrong answers handled?
To what extent is the student role active/passive?
Is student participation welcomed/encouraged/used?
Is the tutor's response to reinforce/reward/ignore?
Are cognitive and/or affective processes used?

3h Is work between classes expected/suggested?
What kind of tasks are set between classes?
Do students complete work between classes?
Is this work commented on/assessed?

3i What assessment methods are used for the course as a whole?
Is assessment compulsory/optional?
Are students involved in the assessment process?

3j To what extent is counselling/guidance provided?
To what extent is information on other/future educational opportunities included?
To what extent is vocational advice available?

4 Evaluation and development

4a *Evaluation of course*
Who is responsible for evaluating the course?
When is the evaluation carried out?
How is evaluation operated? (formal/informal or both?)
What part do tutors play in evaluation?
What part do students play in evaluation?
Are students encouraged to provide feedback?
Is there timetabled feedback and review?
What is evaluated – aims and objectives? target groups? practical arrangements? content? methods? etc.

4b Can modifications be made during the course?
Are modifications made during the course?
Can modifications be made between courses?
Are modifications made between courses?

4c *Evaluation of students*
What student changes are recorded – skills? knowledge? personal development?
What criteria are used to identify success?
Do tutors meet to discuss progress of students?
Are tutor communications about students formal or informal?

4d *Evaluation and development*
Is the course validated by an outside body?
Do the students receive certification?
What criteria and methods are used for certification?

4e *Evaluation and progression*
What do students go on to do after the course?
Is there any follow-up of students after the course?

For how long and to what extent?
Is there any ongoing support for students after the course?
Do many students go on to mixed classes or classes with male tutors?
Are students prepared for this transition?
How do they cope with the transition?

Bibliography

Aaron, J. and Walby, S. (1991) *Out of the Margins: Women's Studies in the 90s.* London, Falmer Press.

Adams, C. (1991) Access through community education. *Adults Learning*, 3(2), 52.

Aird, E. (1980) NOW courses and the changing pattern of adult education. *Studies in Adult Education*, 12(1), 39–44.

Aird, E., Brown, J. and Peacock, G. (1980) The Newcastle/NOW Project. *Adult Education*, 53(1), 32–8.

Arnot, M. (1983) A cloud over co-education. In Walker, S. and Barton, L., *Gender, Class and Education*. London, Falmer Press.

Atkin, G. and Hutchinson, E. (1981) Women in search of education. *Adult Education*, 53(6), 361–5.

Barr, J. (1984) The ways forward. Making our Future: Change in Women's Education. Report of WEA Conference, Durham.

Barratt, M. (1980) *Women's Oppression Today: Problems in Marxist Feminist Analysis*. London, Verso.

Barry, C. (1980) When the kitchen knife is a utensil for liberation. *THES*, no. 441, 8.

Bateson, B. and Bateson, G. (1988) *Women's Education: A Review and Evaluation of Women's Adult Education within the Erdington Area.* (unpublished dissertation).

Bateson, G. (1990) *What Constitutes Quality in One NOW Course?* (unpublished discussion paper).

Belenky, M.F., Clinchy, B.M., Goldberger, N.R. and Terule, J.M. (1986) *Women's Ways of Knowing.* New York, Basic Books.

Bennett, Y. and Carter, D. (1983) *Sidetracked? – A Look at the Careers Advice Given to Fifth Form Girls. Manchester.* Manchester, Equal Opportunities Commission.

Berryman, S. (1992) The FHE White Paper and the FHE Bill – where will it leave access students? *Journal of Access Studies*, 7(1), Spring, 83.

Board of Education (1923) Report by the Consultative Committee on *Differentiation of the Curriculum for Boys and Girls Respectively in Secondary Schools*. London.

Brittain, V. (1933 reprinted 1978) *Testament of Youth*. London, Virago.

Burrow, M. (1985) Wider opportunities for women and work. *Adult Education*, 58(2), 158–62.

Burstyn, J.N. (1980) *Victorian Education and the Ideal of Womanhood*. London, Croom Helm.

Business in the Community (1991) *TECs and Women: Action Issues.* Recommendations from key employers and the EOC, in partnership with Business in the Community, London.

Byrne, E. (1978) *Women and Education*. London, Tavistock.

Calow, M. (1987) Teaching Women's Studies: a personal point of view. *Women's Studies Newsletter*, WEA, April.

Casling, M. (1986) Women's subjects: their place in adult education. *Adult Education*, 59(1), 40–4.

Central Statistical Office (CSO) (1992) *Social Trends*. London, HMSO.

Challude, M. and Lisien-Norman, M. (1987) *The Re-insertion of Women in Working Life: Initiatives and Problems*. Luxembourg, Office for Official Publications of the European Community.

Chetwynd, J. and Hartnett, O. (1978) *The Sex-role System*. London, Routledge and Kegan Paul.

Clark, F. and Hardy, P. (1991) *Return to Work: A Course for Women*. Cambridge, National Extension College.

Coats, M. (1988a) *Consulting Women*. NIACE/Replan (East Midlands), Leicester, NIACE.

Coats, M. (1988b) 'Women returners: A study of mature undergraduates and their educational histories', unpublished PhD thesis. Loughborough University of Technology.

Coats, M. (1989a) *The Case for Women-only Provision and a Women-centred Curriculum*. Women Educating Women Conference Report, Leicester, Open University/National Extension College.

Coats, M. (1989b) Support for women learners: requirements and resources. *Adults Learning*, 1(4), 104–5.

Coats, M. (1990) *Portfolio Preparation: Using the Process with Unwaged Women*. NIACE/ Replan Women's National Planning Group, Leicester, NIACE.

Coats, M. (1991) *Provision for Women in a Context of Change*. NIACE/Replan (Eastern Region) (unpublished).

Coats, M. (1992) Women's education: the background. *Adults Learning*, 3(10), 257.

Coats, M. and McGivney, V. (1992) Editorial. *Adults Learning*, 3(10), 256.

Coats, M., Deere, J. and Goodchild, G. (1988) *The Curriculum and Methodology of Women-only Provision*. FEU (unpublished).

Commission of European Communities (1992) *Newsletter of Community Initiatives: Human Resources*. No. 1, January and No. 2, March.

Crane, S. (1986) *Women and the Voluntary Movement: Learning to Win*. Breaking Our Silence Series, London, WEA.

Davies, M.L. (ed.) (1977) *Life as We Have Known It – by Co-operative Working Women*. London, Virago.

Davin, A. (1978) Imperialism and the cult of motherhood. *History Workshop Journal*, No. 5, 9–65.

Deem, R. (1978) *Women and Schooling*. London, Routledge and Kegan Paul.

Deem, R. (1980) *Schooling for Women's Work*. London, Routledge and Kegan Paul.

Deem, R. (1981) State policy and ideology in the education of women. *British Journal of the Sociology of Education*, 2(2), 131–43.

Deem, R. (1983) Gender, patriarchy and class in the popular education of women. In Walker, S. and Barton, L. *Gender, Class and Education*. London, Falmer Press.

Deem, R. (1984) *Co-education Reconsidered*. Milton Keynes, Open University Press.

Delamont, S. (1980) *Sex Roles and the School*. London, Methuen.

Delamont, S. and Duffin, L. (1978) *The Nineteenth Century Woman*. London, Croom Helm.

Department of Education and Science (1975) *Curricula Differences for Boys and Girls*. Educational Survey 21, London, HMSO.

Department for Education (DE) (1991) *Education Statistics for the United Kingdom*. London, HMSO.

Dobbie, E. (1982) *Returners*. London, National Advisory Centre on Careers for Women.

Dolan, T., Fitzgerald, C., Messer, J. and Townsend, M. (1984) New opportunities for women. *Adult Education,* 57(2), 140–2.

Domino Consultancy (1990) *Returning without Fears.* Shepshed, Domino Consultancy.

Dyhouse, C. (1976) Social ideas and the development of women's education in England 1800–1920. *History of Education,* 5(1), 41–58.

Edwards, J. (1985) *Working-class Adult Education in Liverpool.* Manchester Monograph 25. Centre for Adult and Higher Education, University of Manchester.

EOC (1986) *Signposts – A Guide to Training Opportunities for Women.* Manchester, Equal Opportunities Commission.

EOC (1990) *Training for Women: The Future Imperative.* Discussion Paper. Manchester, Equal Opportunities Commission.

EOC (1991) *Some Facts About Women.* Manchester, Equal Opportunities Commission.

EOC (1992) *Women and Men in Britain.* Manchester, Equal Opportunities Commission.

European Bureau of Adult Education (1992) *Grassroots Education for Women in Europe.* Barcelona, EBAE.

European Commission (1987) Recommendations on vocational training for women. *Official Journal of the European Communities,* December, No. L 342/35.

Fairbairns, J. (1979) *Evaluation of Wider Opportunities for Women (WOW) Courses: Final Report.* Sheffield, Manpower Services Commission.

Faludi, S. (1992) *Backlash: The Undeclared War Against Women.* London, Chatto and Windus.

FEU (1984) *Changing the Focus: Women and FE.* London, FEU Publications.

Flynn, P., Johnson, C., Leiberman, S. and Armstrong, H. (1986) *You're Learning All the Time: Women, Education and Community Work.* Nottingham, Spokesman.

French, J. and French, P. (1984) Gender imbalances in the primary classroom: an interactional account. *Educational Research,* 26(2), 127–36.

French, M. (1992) *The War against Women.* London, Hamish Hamilton.

Gibson, D.R. and Pocock, S.E. (1968) *Married Women Students.* London, University of London, Institute of Education, Bulletin no. 16.

Gray, R. and Hughes, M. (1980) Half our future? *Adult Education,* 52(5), 301–6.

Hakim, C. (1978) Sexual divisions within the labour force. *Department of Employment Gazette,* November, 1264–8, 1278–9.

Hartnett, O., Boden, S. and Fuller, M. (eds) (1979) *Sex-role Stereotyping.* London, Tavistock.

Highet, G. (1986) Gender and education: a study of the ideology and practice of community based women's education as observed in three groups operating in Glasgow. *Studies in the Education of Adults,* 18(2), 118–29.

Hill, L. (1984) New horizons/new opportunities for women. *Adult Education,* 57(3), 262–3.

Hootsmans, H.M. (1980) Educational and employment opportunities for women: main issues in adult education in Europe. *Convergence,* 13(1–2), 79–90.

Hughes, M. (1991a) London took the lead: institutes for women. *Studies in the Education of Adults,* 23(2), 41–55.

Hughes, M. (1991b) Mother's help: policy on the education of mothers. *Adults Learning,* 3(2), 49–51.

Hughes, M. and Kennedy, M. (1983) Breaking out – women in adult education. *Women's Studies International Forum,* 6(3), 261–9.

Hughes, M. and Kennedy, M. (1985) *New Futures: Changing Women's Education.* London, Routledge and Kegan Paul.

Hunt, A. and Rauta, I. (1975) *Fifth-form Girls: Their Hopes for the Future.* London, HMSO.

Hutchinson, E. and Hutchinson, E. (1978) *Later Learning: Fresh Horizons in English Adult Education.* London, Routledge and Kegan Paul.

Hyde, P. (1992) Finance for adult learning: an overview of current provision. *Adults Learning,* 3(9), 228–31.

Jarvis, C. (1992) Keeping them down: women and access provision. *Access and Community Education Studies,* No. 13, 12.

Kelly, J. (1988) Adult education's role in providing women-friendly training and work opportunities. *Adult Education,* 61(1), 20–4.

Kelly, T. (1970) *A History of Adult Education in Britain.* Liverpool, University of Liverpool Press.

Kelly, T. (1983) The historical evolution of adult education in Great Britain. In Tight, M. (ed.) *Educational Opportunities for Adults.* Vol. II. London, Croom Helm.

Kiernan, K. (1992) Men and women at work and at home. In Jowell, R. *et al.* (eds) *British Social Attitudes – The Ninth Report.* Aldershot, Dartmouth Publishing.

Kirk, P. (1982) Return to study provision for women. *Adult Education,* 55(3), 241–8.

Land, H. (1981) *Parity Begins at Home: Women's and Men's Work in the Home and Its Effects on Their Paid Employment.* Manchester, EOC/SSRC Joint Panel.

Licht, B.G. and Dweck, C. (1983) Sex Differences in Achievement Orientations: Consequences for Academic Choices and Attainments. In Marland, M. (ed.) *Sex Differentiation and Schooling.* London, Heinemann.

Lovell, A. (1980a) Fresh horizons: mature students. *Feminist Review,* No. 6, 93–104.

Lovell, A. (1980b) Fresh horizons for some. *Adult Education,* 53(4), 219–24.

McGivney, V. (1992) Women and vocational training: an overview. *Adults Learning,* 3(10), 260.

McLaren, A.T. (1985) *Ambitions and Realizations: Women in Adult Education.* London, Peter Owen.

Mann, F. (1988) *Altered Images.* Breaking Our Silence Series, London, WEA.

Marland, M. (1983) *Sex Differentiation and Schooling.* London, Heinemann.

Marshall, M. and Johnson, C. (1983) New opportunities for women? Women's education in the north of Scotland. *Scottish Journal of Adult Education,* 6(2), 14–22.

Martin, J., Powell, J.P. and Weineke, C. (1981) The experiences of a group of older unqualified women at university. *Women's Studies International Quarterly,* 4(2), 117–31.

Martin, J. and Roberts, C. (1984) *Women and Employment: A Lifetime Perspective.* London, HMSO.

Maynard, L. (1992) Are mature students a problem? *Journal of Access Studies,* 7(1).

Mezirow, J. (1981) A critical theory of adult learning and education. *Adult Education (US),* 32(1), 3–24.

Michaels, R. (1973) *New Opportunities for Women.* Hatfield, Hatfield Polytechnic, Occasional Papers no. 1.

Morgan, V. and Dunn, S. (1981) *Late But in Earnest: Mature Women at University.* CORE, 5(2), Microfiche 6/10 and 7/10. Oxford, Collected Original Resources in Education.

Morris, C. (1986) *Something for Me: Studies of Women in Education.* Manchester, Open College Federation, Paper no. 1.

Moss, W. (1987) *Breaking the Barriers – Eight Case Studies of Women Returning to Learning in North London.* ALFA, London, Polytechnic of North London.

Nashashibi, P. (1980) Education for mature women: the uses of O level English language. *Adult Education,* 52(5), 333–6.

Office of Population Censuses and Surveys, Social Survey Division (1990) *General Household Survey.* London, HMSO.

Oglesby, K.L. (1990) Women's education in Europe: issues for the 90s. *Studies in the Education of Adults*, 22(1), 133–44.

Payne, J. (1991) *Women, Training and the Skills Shortage: The Case for Public Investment.* London, Policy Studies Institute.

Perkin, J. (1984) *It's never too late....* London, Impact Books.

Powell, B. (1992) *Securing Adult Learning – Practical Strategies for Implementing the FHE Act 1992.* Leicester, NIACE.

Pratt, J., Bloomfield, J. and Searle, C. (1984) *Option choice: A Question of Equal Opportunity.* Windsor, NFER–Nelson.

Pravda, G. (1991) *Women-Friendly Approaches to Teaching and Learning: An Overview of Selected Papers.* 'The Student, Community and Curriculum'. OU/ICDE Conference, Cambridge. September.

Purvis, J. (1980) Working class women and adult education in nineteenth century Britain. *History of Education*, 9(3), 193–212.

Replan (1987) *Working with Women newsletter*, Vol 1, 1987; Vol 2, 1988; Vol 3, 1989; Vol 4, 1991. Leicester, NIACE.

Replan (1990) *Women's Education and Change – Briefing Sheets.* NIACE/Replan, Women's National Planning Group, Leicester, NIACE.

Replan (1991a) *A Checklist for Good Practice in Educational Provision for Women.* NIACE/ Replan (West Midlands), Leicester, NIACE.

Replan (1991b) *Women's Education in England and Wales.* NIACE/Replan, Women's National Planning Group, Leicester, NIACE.

Replan (1991c) *Women Learning: Ideas, Approaches and Practical Support.* NIACE/Replan. Leicester, NIACE.

Roberts, Y. (1992) *Mad About Women – Can There Ever Be Fair Play Between the Sexes.* London, Virago.

Sharpe, S. (1984) *Double Identity: The Lives of Working Mothers.* Harmondsworth, Penguin.

Sharpe, T. (1981) New opportunities for women: first steps towards a second chance. *Adult Education*, 53(5), 315–7.

Smithers, A. and Robinson, P. (1989) *Increasing Participation in Higher Education.* London, BP Educational Service.

Spender, D. (1982) *Invisible Women: The Schooling Scandal.* London, Writers and Readers.

Spender, D. and Sarah, E. (1980) *Learning to Lose: Sexism and Education.* London, The Women's Press.

Spendiff, A. (1987) *Maps and Models: Moving Forward with Feminism.* Breaking Our Silence Series, London, WEA.

Sperling, L. (1991) Can the barriers be breached? – mature women's access to HE. *Gender and Education*, 3(2), 199–213.

Stacey, J. (1988) Can there be a feminist ethnography? *Women's Studies International Forum*, 11(2), 21–7.

Stanley, L. and Wise, S. (1983) *Breaking out – Feminist Consciousness and Feminist Research.* London, Routledge and Kegan Paul.

Stoney, S. and Reid, M. (1980) *Further Opportunities in Focus – A Study of Bridging Courses for Women.* London, NFER/FEU.

Stoney, S. and Reid, M. (1981) *Balancing the Equation – A Study of Women and Science and Technology within FE.* London, NFER/FEU.

Sullerot, E. (1987) *The Diversification of Vocational Choices for Women.* Luxembourg, Office for Official Publications of the European Community.

Sutherland, M. (1981) *Sex Bias in Education*. Oxford, Basil Blackwell.

Taking Liberties Collective (1989) *Learning the Hard Way – Women's Oppression in Men's Education*. Women in Society Series, London, Macmillan.

Tallantyre, F. (1985) *Women at the Crossroads: Ten Years of NOW Courses in Northern District*. Breaking Our Silence Series, London, WEA.

Thompson, J. (ed.) (1980) *Adult Education for a Change*. London, Hutchinson.

Thompson, J. (1983) *Learning Liberation: Women's Response to Men's Education*. London, Croom Helm.

Title, C.K. and Denker, E.R. (1977) Re-entry women: a selective review of educational process, career choice and interest measurement. *Review of Educational Research*, 47(4), 531–84.

Walker, L. and Barton, L. (eds) (1983) *Gender, Class and Education*. London, Falmer Press.

Warwick, J. and Williamson, A. (1989) *Equal Opportunities (Gender) Policy and Practice in Colleges of Further Education*. FEU Research Project 505 (unpublished).

Weil, S.W. (1986) Non-traditional learners within traditional HE institutions: discovery and disappointment. *Studies in Higher Education*, 11(3), 219–35.

Whyld, J. (1983) *Sexism in the Secondary Curriculum*. London, Harper and Row.

Willis, L. and Daisley, J. (1990) *Springboard – Women's Development Workbook*. Stroud, Hawthorn Press.

Wilson, V. (1985) Wider Opportunities for Women: a case study approach. *Adult Education*, 57(4), 310–4.

Women's National Commission (1984) *The Other Half of Our Future*. London, Cabinet Office, Women's National Commission.

Women's National Commission (1991) *Women Returners: Employment Potential – An Agenda For Action*. London, Cabinet Office, Women's National Commission.

Women Returners' Network (1987) *Returning to Work: Education and Training for Women* (1st edn). Harlow, Longmans.

Women Returners' Network (1992) *Returning to Work: Education and Training for Women* (6th edn). Ware, MJ Publishing.

Woolsey, L.K. and McBain, L.L. (1987) Issues of power and powerlessness in all-women groups. *Women's Studies International Forum*, 10(6), 579–88.

Index

The Society for Research into Higher Education

The Society for Research into Higher Education exists to stimulate and co-ordinate research into all aspects of higher education. It aims to improve the quality of higher education through the encouragement of debate and publication on issues of policy, on the organization and management of higher education institutions, and on the curriculum and teaching methods.

The Society's income is derived from subscriptions, sales of its books and journals, conference fees and grants. It receives no subsidies, and is wholly independent. Its individual members include teachers, researchers, managers and students. Its corporate members are institutions of higher education, research institutes, professional, industrial and governmental bodies. Members are not only from the UK, but from elsewhere in Europe, from America, Canada and Australasia, and it regards its international work as amongst its most important activities.

Under the imprint *SRHE & Open University Press*, the Society is a specialist publisher of research, having some 45 titles in print. The Editorial Board of the Society's Imprint seeks authoritative research or study in the above fields. It offers competitive royalties, a highly recognizable format in both hardback and paperback and the world-wide reputation of the Open University Press.

The Society also publishes *Studies in Higher Education* (three times a year), which is mainly concerned with academic issues, *Higher Education Quarterly* (formerly *Universities Quarterly*), mainly concerned with policy issues, *Research into Higher Education Abstracts* (three times a year), and *SRHE News* (four times a year).

The Society holds a major annual conference in December, jointly with an institution of higher education. In 1991, the topic was 'Research and Higher Education in Europe', with the University of Leicester. In 1992, it was 'Learning to Effect' with Nottingham Trent University, and in 1993, 'Governments and the Higher Education Curriculum: Evolving Partnerships' at the University of Sussex in Brighton. Future conferences include in 1994, 'The Student Experience' at the University of York.

The Society's committees, study groups and branches are run by the members. The groups at present include:

Teacher Education Study Group
Continuing Education Group
Staff Development Group
Excellence in Teaching and Learning

Benefits to members

Individual

Individual members receive:

* *SRHE News*, the Society's publications list, conference details and other material included in mailings.
* Greatly reduced rates for *Studies in Higher Education and Higher Education Quarterly*.
* A 35% discount on all Open University Press & SRHE publications.
* Free copies of the Precedings – commissioned papers on the theme of the Annual Conference.
* Free copies of *Research into Higher Education Abstracts*.
* Reduced rates for conferences.
* Extensive contacts and scope for facilitating initiatives.
* Reduced reciprocal memberships.

Corporate

Corporate members receive:

* All benefits of individual members, plus
* Free copies of *Studies in Higher Education*.
* Unlimited copies of the Society's publications at reduced rates.
* Special rates for its members e.g. to the Annual Conference.

Membership details: SRHE, 344–354 Gray's Inn Road, London, WC1X 8BP, UK, Tel: 071 837 7880
Catalogue: SRHE & Open University Press, Celitic Court, 22 Ballmoor, Buckingham MK18 1XW. Tel: (0280) 823388

WOMEN RETURNING TO HIGHER EDUCATION

Gillian Pascall and Roger Cox

This book draws on interviews with forty-three mature women students at two East Midlands institutions of higher education. Women returners gave eloquent accounts of constraints and opportunities, aspirations about careers, anxieties and excitement about change. Just over half were traced and re-interviewed eight years later. These later interviews focus on public and private views of the impact of education: accounts of subsequent careers, and re-assessments of the educational experience in terms of personal self-fulfilment.

The work is a rich account of the way women perceive their educational experiences drawing on their own interpretations. It also connects with several theoretical traditions: work on why adults return to education, on women's relationship to education systems, on the relationship between women's paid and unpaid work. As these students were a pioneering group for a much wider expansion in higher education, the book is a timely contribution to debates about widening access.

Contents

192pp   0 335 19055 3 (Paperback)   0 335 19056 1 (Hardback)

WOMEN IN EDUCATIONAL MANAGEMENT

Jenny Ozga (ed.)

This book provides us with women managers' own vivid accounts of their varied career paths into educational management and of their day-to-day experiences as women in management posts. Jenny Ozga and her contributors explore the issues which develop both from a recognition of women's minority status in educational management, and from the idea that women may manage differently from men. By offering a series of accounts by women managers at all levels in the education system, *Women in Educational Management* hopes to encourage other women to consider the possibility of a career in educational management. By describing some of the problems faced by women managers it will help others to identify the barriers to progress, and consider strategies for overcoming them. Finally, by presenting positive arguments for women as managers, it will help combat stereotypical images of management as a 'masculine' activity.

Contents
Introduction: in a different mode – Black women in educational management – The community education coordinator – The chief education officer – The secondary head – The secondary deputy – The primary head – The head of department in teacher education – From HMI to polytechnic director – A training initiative – Gender issues in management training – Index.

Contributors
Harry Gray, Ros Harrison, Margaret Maden, Jenny Ozga, Pauline Perry, Mollie Roach, Maureen Sedgwick, Nancy Traquair, Cas Walker, Joan Whitehead, Jane Williams.

128pp   0 335 09340 X (Paperback)

GENDER AND SUBJECT IN HIGHER EDUCATION

Kim Thomas

Despite the growing number of studies of gender in education, the topic of gender in higher education has often been ignored. This far-ranging book attempts to redress the balance by an exploration of a number of related issues: why women and men tend to specialize in different subject areas; the experience of being a woman in a 'man's' subject and a man in a 'woman's' subject; whether higher education plays a part in reproducing gender inequality. In particular, the author focuses on the arts/science divide; taking two representative subjects, physics and English, she looks at the way each is constructed by lecturers and students, and the relationship between these constructions and the social construction of gender. She argues that students choose which subject to study on the basis of certain qualities these subjects are seen to hold, and that these qualities have close connections with beliefs about 'masculinity' and 'femininity'. Most students develop a subject loyalty, reinforced by studying the discipline in higher education, but this subject loyalty can be challenged or reinforced by a student's sense of gender identity. The author argues that the boundaries between different disciplines are often artificial and limiting, and for this reason she also looks at attempts in polytechnics to remove interdisciplinary barriers, asking whether subjects such as communications and physical science provide a challenge to traditional university subjects like English and physics. The author concludes that universities have, on the whole, been complacent about the issue of gender inequality and suggests that a fresh look at current practices is overdue.

This book will be a thought-provoking read for anybody who teaches in higher education, as well as for those specializing in the areas of gender and education and women's studies.

Contents
The question of gender – Feminism and education – The two cultures – Constructing science – Constructing humanities – Gender identity and science students – Gender identity and humanities students – Conclusion – References – Index.

208pp   0 335 09271 3 (Paperback)   0 335 09272 1 (Hardback)